SALTWATER VILLAGE

UNIVERSITY OF CAMBRIDGE
BOARD OF CONTINUING EDUCATION

MADINGLEY HALL
CAMBRIDGE

SALTWATER VILLAGE

by

MARGARET LEATHER

Introduction by John Leather

TERENCE DALTON LIMITED
LAVENHAM . SUFFOLK
1977

Published by
TERENCE DALTON LIMITED

ISBN 0 86138 022 3

First Impression 1977
Second Impression 1983

Text Photoset in 11/12pt. Baskerville

Printed in Great Britain at
THE LAVENHAM PRESS LIMITED
LAVENHAM   SUFFOLK

Contents

Index of Illustrations

For "Rowhedgers", old and new.

ACKNOWLEDGEMENTS AND NOTES

The author's thanks are due to many old friends from Rowhedge who have helped with reminiscence and prompted memory. Particular assistance was received from Audrey and Wilfrid Ainger, Jack Barnard, Susannah Bedford, Jack Wilkin, Bessie Willsmore, Captain Charles Watson, O.B.E., Bessie Clark, James Theobald and Jess Carter. I am grateful to my daughter-in-law, Doris Leather, for typing the manuscript and to my son John for encouraging its writing and contributing many photographs. Excellent photographs have also been contributed from the historical collections of Roger M. Smith and Dr N. Vashon Baker. Others are by the late Douglas Went, the noted east coast marine photographer. The Essex Record staff were very helpful with the selection of maps.

Throughout the book money values have been expressed in pounds, shillings and pence, contemporary with its period.

Margaret Leather,
Valkyrie Cottages,
Rowhedge. 1973.

Rowhedge heyday, winter 1908. High Street from opposite Pearson's Quay. A smack alongside the Anchor Quay on left. Laid up yachts line the river wall above the village, as far as the "first bridge". A yacht is on the slipway in Houston's yard, in centre background. The ferryboat lies at the ferry hard landing, where two cottages hide the *Anchor* public house, beyond.

Introduction

THIS is a first hand account of life in the Essex maritime village of Rowhedge during its late Victorian and early twentieth century heyday, recalled from the author's childhood and early life, and covering from about 1898 to 1920, but often extending well beyond this by earlier traditions remembered and older stories retold, as well as other sources of information.

Rowhedge is on the west bank of the river Colne in north-east Essex, about four miles south of the small port of Colchester, almost opposite but slightly upstream from the larger village of Wivenhoe. It is an old settlement, undoubtedly sited on this bend of the Colne because of the natural tidal scour, which gives good depth of water close to its quays.

Rowhedge is believed to have originated as a waterside hamlet, also sometimes known as "Hedge Row", within the parish of East Donyland. As the population grew, it eclipsed that of the rural parish and in the mid-nineteenth century the new church and school were sited in Rowhedge, though they remain prefixed by "East Donyland". By then Rowhedge extended along its waterside High Street and, in parts, up the shoulder of the little hill which shelters it from westerly winds. Its fleet of smacks sailed to the North Sea fisheries and its wooden shipbuilders launched merchant and fishing vessels for owners in Rowhedge and other ports. At that time it was a place of transhipment for goods for Colchester and for ballasting the ships which discharged them.

The population was almost wholly maritime and activity increased until by the 1870's about 900 inhabitants were dependent on owning and manning 33 large smacks averaging 23 tons each, fishing the North Sea and all round the British coasts. Its merchant ships were also trading coastwise and overseas and Philip Mosely Sainty's shipyard was launching 200 tonners, brigs and barques, while Harris Brothers were building many smacks and refitting the increasing numbers of yachts laying up at Rowhedge each winter as skippers and crews from the village began to gain yachting eminence, particularly in yacht racing, where their seamanship and success provided modest prosperity for Rowhedge, financing the building of many smacks and the greater part of the village houses until 1914.

The period 1890 to 1914 was Rowhedge's maritime heyday and on 31st January, 1896, Mrs Leather was born Margaret Barnard, daughter of Captain James Barnard, a Rowhedge fishing smack owner and yacht captain, and a

11

granddaughter of the noted smack owner, salvager (and occasionally smuggler) Thomas Barnard. Her brothers and uncles were all yacht captains, sailors or shipbuilders. Two of them captained yachts which raced for the America's Cup.

Her book expresses vividly what it was like to grow up in a small seafaring community of the time, her accurate social observation giving the pattern of the year and seasons in the village; how people lived; what they ate and wore; how they cooked and entertained themselves; the children's games and pastimes; village Christmasses and regattas; the domestic background to the days of sail with the hopes and fears of the fisheries; anxiety for ships overdue; the cheerful managing on small and uncertain incomes and many now almost forgotten facts of local life.

The quiet respectability of self-contained village life is set against the backcloth of the ever-changing enterprise and uncertainty of seafaring; a portrait of a community with faith in God, in itself, in the rector, the doctor, the British Navy and the power of the Union Jack.

Village characters abound; old Zike the birdcatcher; Gooseberry Lil and Captain Splasher, the elegant tramps; Mrs Rose and her travelling fair; Jack Spitty the smuggler; the immaculate Captain Walford and his smart steam yacht *Walrus*; old Thompson the step dancer; Captain Powell and his village crew who had sailed around the world; Pincushion the paraffin oil man, and many more.

There are old local legends; the Rowhedge pirate hanged and buried at the crossroads with a stake through his body which had sprouted into an ancient oak tree; the phantom "old man who shakes his chains" at night along the path by Mill Creek, conveniently to scare the inquisitive who might investigate a smuggler's favourite landing place; the clashing swords of ghostly cavaliers, duelling to death on the last night of each year in an old inn room.

She brings to life the tramp of seaboots echoing on winter mornings above the chirrup of blocks. Tall topmasts rearing above the rooftops and tons of silver sprats on the quays. Lofts full of nets, ropes and sails. Gardens with yachts and smack-boats amongst the geraniums and sprats smoking in little wooden houses at the bottom.

Cheesecutter caps and seaboots along the quays, flowered hats and shawls along High Street, which internationally famous racing captains paced in one part while the hands walked another; picture hats and sailor suits in the bluebell woods; the glossy brown horses ploughing fields by the river where fishing smacks and barges, square-riggers and racing yachts, lifted their canvas. Smells of pitch and paint; wood shavings and oakum picked by little fingers. Men splicing ropes and bending sails; a maritime world where female participation stopped at the quays, except on regatta days, or the rare day's outing "down river".

But the sea early wove its way into the children's lives; skipping ropes of best yacht manilla; hoops made in the shipsmith's forge; mud ovens on the sea wall; sea shells for scales; drums and penny whistles salvaged from a wreck; signal rockets for Guy Fawkes night; a tartan bonnet brought from Scotland after a successful summer's yachting.

There are minor dramas and excitements; a birthday party interrupted by news of the family smack ashore in a North Sea gale; the locally built seaplane which became an aeroplane but wouldn't fly as either; the traction engine which bogged down at the flower show; how the soldiers marched off to Gallipoli; when the German Gothas bombed the Essex coast; the King comes to the village; the first local motor car; processions; treats; fairs; the Essex earthquake; the fisherman and the battleship's captain; silks and pianos from a wreck; the day the Zeppelin crashed.

Evocative, nostalgic but accurate social history written from experience with understanding, it will stand as a record of the domestic background to a now vanished way of English life in which everyone is increasingly interested.

This book commences when the village had about 1,100 inhabitants. Most of the male population were engaged fishing in Rowhedge-owned sailing smacks during the winter and in summer served as captains, mates and hands, (as seamen were known) in racing, cruising and steam yachts. A few seafarers shipped as seamen in ocean-going steamships during the winter and some young Rowhedge men were apprenticed in sailing ships at that period, in the hope of obtaining a mate's and eventually a master's certificate. Some attained considerable competence as navigators.

Harris Brothers continued to design, build, repair and refit yachts of all sizes and many types in their yard "Down Street" which included Sainty's old shipyard site. At the upper end of the waterside John A. Houston carried on the same type of work in what had been Puxley's yard and also built some commercial craft such as dumb barges and launches, besides steam pinnaces for the Admiralty and lifeboats. These yards employed many shipwrights and apprentices, riggers and painters from the village and some from Wivenhoe. Similarly, other Rowhedge men found work in the Wivenhoe ship and yacht yards. There were ancillary activities such as shoemaking and tailoring for yacht crews and the village's two firms of yacht decorators, Scrutton and Sons and Mr Pearson, were in demand.

Although its seafarers voyaged around the world, Rowhedge's female population, children and old people had little mobility, in the manner of the time. A few inhabitants owned horses and traps but for most it was "shanks pony" or perhaps the carrier's cart for a journey to Colchester or the railway for a rare visit to London or elsewhere.

Land communication from Rowhedge was by road to Colchester and the adjoining villages of Fingringhoe, to the south-east, Old Heath to the north-west and Berechurch to the west, beyond the woods and heath. A rowing ferry operated across the Colne to a hard on the Wivenhoe side, whence a stony road led to Wivenhoe, a larger village of similar interests, having a station on the Great Eastern railway line from Clacton-on-Sea to Liverpool Street Station, London, passing through Colchester and with a junction branch line to Brightlingsea, a fishing and yachting town of about 5,000 inhabitants on a creek at the entrance to the Colne.

The layout of the older part of Rowhedge has changed little since the period of this book. The principal street is still High Street, which runs parallel with the river Colne and stretches from the "Black Gate" in the south to the "Marsh Stile Gate" at its northern end. This is the oldest part of the village and streets lead off it, up the hillside to the west. From the south these are: Albion Street, Post Office Lane (a cul-de-sac), Church Street (usually known as Church Lane) Regent Street, Darkhouse Lane (a cul-de-sac) and Head Street. The High Street continued northwards to the brook as "the New Road" (now renamed Marsh Crescent) and eventually to the road up to the "Town Fields" (now named Rowhedge Road).

Other roads continued from these: Albion Street forked at the top into Jubilee (now Parkfield Street) and Paget Road, which joined with Taylors Road. Church Lane leads to Church Hill, which also has a junction with Taylors Road. Regent Street joined with these at its top and Taylors Road now continues to the top of Head Street. Head Street has two roads leading off its north side, Chapel Street and "The Cut" (now named West Street). The road to the heath which led from the top of Head Street was known simply as "up the road" but was later named Rectory Road.

Paths led from the ends of Jubilee (Parkfield Street) and the end of Church Hill across a field (now a recreation ground), to the "Old Churchyard" adjoining the Fingringhoe Road, with a branch off to "Granny Stairs" on "the road". Another path led from the path near the churchyard, towards the heath and the Fingringhoe Road. This was called the "Nursery Path", because of the irregularly shaped piece of land enclosed between it and the Fingringhoe Road. On this grew a stand of fine Douglas Fir trees which were felled in 1942.

A path led from the Black Gate, across the lower end of fields, to the side of Mill Creek, leading to Fingringhoe Mill and into that village, to the south. Another path led from the Marsh Stile Gate at the top of High Street, along the river wall to the Hythe at Colchester. All these paths were much used until very recent times.

Seafaring, particularly fishing and yachting, was then a very insecure occupation and ship and yacht building little better. As almost all Rowhedge inhabitants had to work hard for any advancement they gained, there was little if any snobbery and a spirit of helpfulness existed amongst the villagers. The author commented, "There was a great deal of poverty, but in spite of that people led more contented lives and home life was much deeper than it seems today. The tempo of life was much slower and the motor had yet to make itself felt; that being so the world was a better place."

The First World War shook and confused the established order of village life, as it did most communities of the combatant nations. Yachting and fishing declined between 1919 and 1939, when the Rowhedge Ironworks Company's shipbuilding yard became the villagers' mainstay of employment. During the 1930s and into the 1960s, large fields to the south west and west of the village were excavated for sand and ballast, to be processed near the river, and sent off, at first in sailing and motor barges and later predominantly by road transport. Huge scars were left in an otherwise pastoral landscape by these pits but they have at least saved two sides of Rowhedge from speculative building, the river Colne protecting the other. Over the years the pits have gradually reverted to nature, with grasses and trees.

The closing of the shipyard in 1964 was a great blow to Rowhedge employment and pride but the Lower Yard, once Harris Brothers, continues to build and repair yachts and R.N.L.I. lifeboats under the ownership of Ian Brown Ltd. Some small yachts are kept at Rowhedge and many visit its quays during the summer, when the village regatta is amongst the most popular in the area.

Rowhedge preserves its identity by the belt of farmland between it and once rural Old Heath, now a suburb of Colchester and, further west, by the extensive "government land" owned by the Army for training and including the Donyland Wood and Heath. Long may these barriers remain unspoiled.

John Leather,
Isle of Wight.
April 1977.

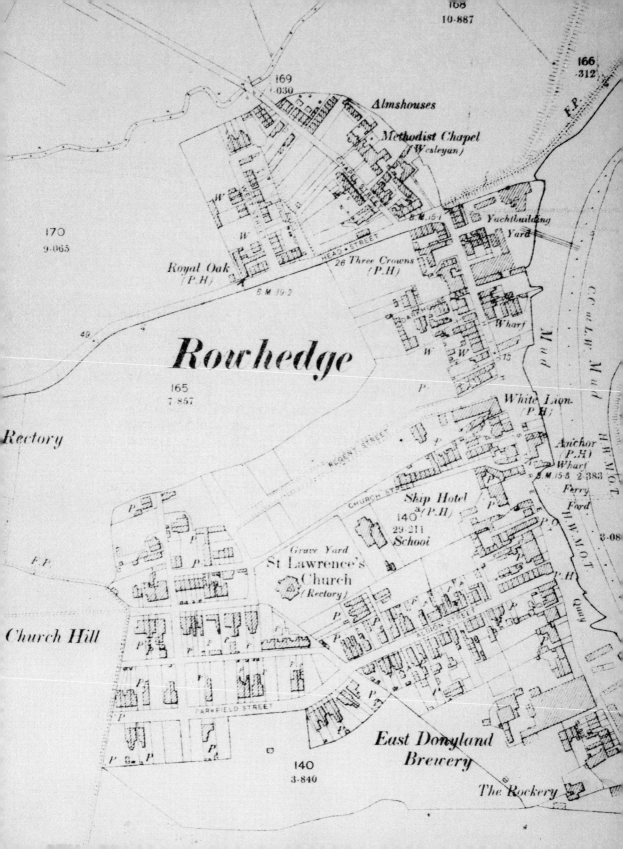

168
10·887

166
·312

169
·030

Almshouses

Methodist Chapel
(Wesleyan)

170
9·065

W

W

B.M. 15·1

Yachtbuilding
Yard

HEAD STREET

Royal Oak
(P.H)

B.M. 39·2

26 *Three Crowns*
(P.H)

W

Wharf

Rowhedge

165
7·857

49

P.

White Lion
(P.H)

Rectory

REGENT STREET

Anchor
(P.H)
Wharf

B.M. 15·5   2·383

Ferry
Ford

CHURCH STREET

Ship Hotel
140ᵃ *(P.H)*

29·211
School

3·08

F.P.

P

P

P

P

P

Grave Yard
St Lawrence's
Church
(Rectory)

P.

P.

P.H.

Quay

Church Hill

ALBION STREET

PARKFIELD STREET

P

P

P

P

P

East Donyland
Brewery

140
3·840

The Rockery

CHAPTER ONE

Upstreet

I WAS born at Rowhedge in a house close to the quays at the upper end of High Street. From a small child I was observant of the tides, wind and weather and all that they meant when one's father and brothers were all seafarers. Life was not very easy in those days, but there, life never has been easy, has it? Pleasures were simple and above all the great love within families was very strong.

A recital of family connections is usually uninteresting to those not related, but I feel that before starting my story I had better set out the immediate relationships. My father, James Barnard, owned the fishing smack *Beatrice* and in summer was captain of cruising yachts. He was one of the sons of Thomas Barnard, a noted Rowhedge smack owner who married Jane James, also from Rowhedge, My mother, Elizabeth, was a daughter of Captain George Cranfield, another yacht skipper and smack owner of the village. His wife Sarah was one of the Wordley family of East Donyland; I remember her well as a person with a keen memory of village history, people and events. She died in 1914 aged ninety-six.

I was the youngest child of a family of seven. My sisters were Hettie and Elizabeth and brothers George (known as Tim), James, William and John (Jack). George was a shipwright, but had also been to sea; the others were all seafarers. My father's brothers Turner, John, Benjamin, James, Arthur and Robert were all owners of smacks and captains of yachts: his sisters were Julia and Susan. My mother's six brothers, George, Lemon, Stephen, William, Jonathan (John) and Richard were also smack owners and captains of racing yachts.

This sort of family background was normal in the Rowhedge of that time, when everyone there looked towards the sea for their living. I want to reconstruct life and scenes in the village as they were during my young life. There is a great variety of things to be seen and told and it will be best if we walk its streets and countryside to discover them.

Rowhedge's main street was High Street, which ran parallel with the river. It had no pavements as in parts it was far too narrow, so we all walked in the road. It stretched from the Black Gate at the southern end to the Marsh Style Gate in the north so will you walk with me along its entire length, as seen by me in my very young days. Starting our walk from the Black Gate, upwards, and going on our way slowly, we would see firstly Cat Island, unknown as such now except to Rowhedge's older inhabitants. It was a fork of land jutting out at the lower end of the shipyard. Two cottages stood there and it was here that my grandfather, Thomas Barnard, lived for many years and was reputed to have been the owner of Cat Island at the time. It was incorporated in the lower yard of yachtbuilders Ian Brown Ltd. The two cottages have been demolished and a new house has been built on the site, known as Rook Bay House; Rook Bay is a small dock adjoining the south-east side of Cat Island.

Grandfather Barnard died the year I was born but I know he was one of the village's most noted seafarers, owning several large fishing smacks, the *Prince of Orange*, the *Thomas and Mary* and the *New Unity*, largest of all. Like most Rowhedge smack owners of his generation, grandfather and his crews fished all over the North Sea, off the coasts of Holland and Belgium, frequently dredging the deep sea oysters and scallops. They also trawled for fish and sometimes went spratting, though the smacks were rather large for this. Sometimes they sailed down the English Channel to fish off the French coast and at other times round Land's End to dredge oysters off the coast of Wales and in the Solway Firth. They also dredged off the east coast of Scotland. Some fast smacks were in demand as fish carriers and grandfather sometimes carried fresh salmon from the west coast of Ireland to Liverpool and from the west coast of Scotland; also, it was said, lobsters from Norway to England.

Grandfather was well-known as a pilot on the east coast and several large Rowhedge smacks worked as pilots in the days before the official pilotage service was organised and when there were few navigational marks. Like many local people of the time, grandfather Barnard was reputed to be involved in smuggling and I have no doubt this was so. Certainly there were very large cellars under his house, which were probably put to good use. However, he was best known as one of the local smack owners who excelled in rescuing survivors from the many ships wrecked on the coast in the winter gales. The big smacks were always on the lookout to render assistance to wrecks and ships in difficulties. Often there were stirring rescues at great risk to the salvagers. It was reckoned that grandfather and his smacks had saved over 900 lives in this way and he and his sons were several times "chaired" through the streets at Harwich, where they sometimes landed shipwrecked crews, carried shoulder high through cheering crowds at the quayside. The other part of salvaging, as it was called, was getting a wrecked ship's cargo and anything of value from her, often at risk of life and certainly extremely hard work, officially to be landed for the local Receiver of Wrecks but sometimes to be run ashore in secret. Some crews did well out of well-known wrecks. The largest was the German ship *Deutchesland* which, besides carrying passengers, many of whom were drowned, also had a large mixed cargo, pianos and silks being amongst the things brought ashore.

My grandfather, Thomas Barnard, seated on the quay near his smack. He was smack owner, fisherman, salvager, pilot and occasionally smuggler.

Salvaging had almost died out before I was born but the memories remained as well as reminders. When Captain John Bartholomew's wife went to church it was said the rustle of her silk petticoats could be very plainly heard and there was fine cutlery and glassware in many households.

Grandfather Barnard retired from the sea after his big smack *New Unity* was herself wrecked in a blizzard, but he evidently continued to keep an eye on all which went on along the waterside. Although he no longer went to sea, he continued to wear his sou-wester hat and, often, his oilskin coat, until his death in 1896.

Sometimes tragedy struck at the salvagers and many were drowned. One Rowhedge seafaring family had a big smack which was usually skippered by the father. One wild winter's day when he was at home ill he ordered two of his sons to take her to sea to seek salvage, despite the pleadings of his distracted wife. The smack was lost and the sons drowned. His wife could not bring herself to continue to live with him, but always saw that his cooked meals were sent in and that his house was cleaned. It was said that two of his daughters were capable of taking a smack to sea alone, and they were larger than the smacks of later years. Another son owned two big smacks and was mate of a yacht in summer.

When I was very young a number of very large old smacks lay in Rook Bay. These were some of the big old salvagers owned in the village which by then had become almost out of date for the fisheries, needing too many men to man them for the poor return their catches brought. When salvaging became less frequent, many had been laid up and these were some of the survivors. One was William Bartholomew's *Alexandra*, another was the old *Prince of Orange*, then owned by my Uncle Turner Barnard, and the third was the big black *Morgan*, owned by my Uncle John O. Barnard. I remember little about them except that the owners used to walk downstreet to pump them out occasionally. At the south side of Rook Bay, over the river wall, was a fenced-off, small marshy meadow where yachts' masts and dinghies were placed to be rubbed down and varnished.

Walking back into the street again we find the yachtyard on our right. In the early part of this century it was owned by the Harris family, who lived in a house named The Rockery, opposite. The Harris family had the yard since about 1865 when I believe Mr Peter T. Harris and his sons, Enos and later John, started building smacks and yachts at the lower yard, now it is Ian Brown Ltd. and still a yachtyard where men build and repair wooden craft.

Harris's were renowned for their thorough workmanship, building many cruising yachts including the *Firecrest*, which in later years was sailed round the world by the Frenchman Alain Gerbault. They also built some racing yachts besides many fishing smacks of various tonnage. It was in this yard that the fishing smack *Wonder*, CK40* was lengthened amidships by six feet which

*Fishing registration number CK indicating Colchester as port of registry.

Part of Harris Brothers yachtyard. A smack on the hard at left. Smack on the slipway is James Carter's *Wonder*, being lengthened six feet amidships. A yacht is building under a roof (centre background) and a newly fitted out yawl lies at the quay. The rigging loft door is open. Daniells brewery at right.

The yacht *Firecrest* built by Harris Brothers. Captain Philip James of Rowhedge on deck. In later years she was sailed around the world by the French yachtsman Alain Gerbault.

I believe was considered quite a feat of planning and workmanship. Owned and sailed by Captain Jim Carter, she was always spoken of as a lucky smack and usually, when trawling and stowboating, her catches beat almost all the many others fishing from Rowhedge.

In winter many large yachts were laid up at this yard which meant plenty of work from autumn to late spring, in addition to new yachts being built and smacks repaired. Many famous yachts were slipped and refitted; Lord Dunraven's cruising ketch *Cariad*, Mr Stamp's steam yacht *Walrus*, and the *Gwendoline* are the ones I remember most but there were scores of others, large and small. The bows of hauled-up yachts sometimes stuck out over the High Street, with men working on them. Big capstans hauled the slips up and there were huge crane-like sheerlegs on the quays to lift the masts in and out, and the engines and boilers of the steam yachts.

The yard employed many shipwrights and apprentices, besides riggers and painters. My brother George (Tim) Barnard was an apprentice shipwright there. Evidently at first he didn't like it very much, so he ran away, no one knew where, until my father, who was searching for him, went down to Brightlingsea and found him. He had got himself a berth in a yacht there and when my father saw him, he was up the yacht's mast, scraping it. Of course he was brought home right away and continued with his apprenticeship at Harris's, and that was that.

In winter, after the workmen had left the yard when the bell rang for dinner time, Mr Harris used to come hurrying out with some of the yacht captains; perhaps Captain Bartholomew Smith of the *Cariad* and Captain Henry Sebborn of the steam yacht *Gwendoline*, smartly dressed in their pilot coats and cheesecutter hats, and Captain Ben Walford of the steam yacht *Walrus* swaggering along, in an immaculately cut suit, sometimes even carrying a cane and gloves. So smart was he that villagers said when he was in company with the owner it was difficult to know which was which! It was said in the village that the only occasion when Captain Walford appeared ruffled was when the *Walrus*, on her way to Holland, was run into and nearly sunk in the North Sea by a German battleship. However, she was repaired and reappeared, as smart as ever.

A few small yachts were also kept at Rowhedge. The village doctor, Dr Kevern, was a keen amateur yachtsman and owned the little white cutter yacht *Narcissus* which he raced in the local regattas with my Uncle George Cranfield as skipper and the late Fred Gould as boy. He cruised in her when possible and later bought the smart black cutter *Blonde*, which was such a great favourite of his that he wished when he died that she should be burned at sea with his body on board, but this unusual burial did not take place.

On the opposite side of the road, at the upper end of the yard, were several houses and three very old cottages, long since gone. Then on to

Dr G. Travers Kevern, the village doctor, was a keen amateur yachtsman, owning the 39ft cutter *Narcissus*. Here she is beating to windward in a regatta.

Daniells Brewery which covered a large area with brick buildings, now all but one demolished, the rest of the site being partly a garage and partly built over. Many of us children looked through the grilles in the outside doors to see the furnaces burning brightly. Sailing barges brought barley and other cargoes to the brewery, unloading at the quay before it and which is still known as the Brewery Quay. The little crane which unloaded or loaded them with barrels, is also still there and used by the yachtyard.

The Brewery at Rowhedge must have been the cradle of the Daniells firm and the family must have lived here in the late nineteenth century. There is no trace now of their house at Weir Lane near Donyland Wood, but the site is still remembered by some as Daniells Garden. Later the family built Heath House, not far from the *Ipswich Arms*, which is still a lovely house, standing far back from the road. The gardens were beautifully kept and I remember that Miss Daniell was organist at Rowhedge church for a time. But time marched on, and the family moved to West Bergholt, where their new brewery had opened, and the one at Rowhedge was shut.

A few more steps will bring us in full view of the river and its quays and the houses on the opposite side of High Street where my uncle, Captain John Cranfield and his family, lived at Vine Cottage, a double-fronted house with a small cottage attached. Vine Cottage (unnamed today) had large front and back gardens carefully attended by his son Stephen. There you would find a succession of brightly coloured flowers with a large rose bed in the centre; vegetables of all kinds in the back garden and also a wonderful display of cactus dahlias.

The next house is larger than most. I was told several years ago that it was built for and lived in by one of the sons of the Havens family who are or were Lord of the Manor of East Donyland. This house was occupied later by Mr Octavious Blyth who was in charge of the brewery, presumably as manager. I remember standing in a crowd outside the house after the results of an election in the Harwich Division, waiting to see H. K. Newton (Conservative) step out with Mr and Mrs Blyth on to the top of one of the bay windows, which they did eventually in response to the cheering crowds outside. That year H. K. Newton was returned Member of Parliament for the Harwich Division with a large majority over his Liberal opponent, Levy Lever. There were plenty of blue rosettes in Rowhedge at that election and at previous elections too. I think it is safe to say, politically speaking, at that time Rowhedge was predominately "true blue".

After a row of houses is the entrance to Albion Street, which stretches up the hill, flanked on one side by a shop and on the other by the *Albion Hotel*. My uncle, John O. Barnard, kept the shop (then a butcher's) and the *Albion Hotel* at the same time. A very shrewd man was he with piercing, eagle-like eyes. His wife was just the opposite; in fact her manner was that of a sophisticated Victorian lady.

Of course, along with his brothers, Uncle "John O" as he was known, spent his early life at sea in one or another of my grandfather's smacks and it is my opinion that each one of them in their early years had no alternative, no choice, so they all had to rough it. Sometimes it was fishing, or salvaging when the gales were raging; at other times it was smuggling, and many more Rowhedge boats were in it. Later he owned the big smack *Morgan*. After he

Looking up High Street. *Albion Hotel* at left with sailors standing outside. Pearson's and Albion Quays at right, with a smack alongside, laid up for the summer. Rowhedge Ironworks shipyard in centre right background.

had kept *The Albion* for a few more years "John O" retired and for a short time lived with his wife in one of his houses "up Jubilee" in the upper part of Rowhedge, but soon moved to Walton-on-Naze and opened a general shop in the High Street. I think it was stocked with practically everything one could think of and evidently it was a money spinner. He eventually owned quite a lot of property there including half a street of houses, together with the house and shop he occupied and four houses in Rowhedge.

Moving along again we pass Stone Alley and two cottages. In the further one Mrs Dan James kept her pork butcher's shop in the front room. Today these two cottages have been made into one and attractively modernised. Adjoining it is Quay House which to my mind is the outstanding house of the village. I must confess that over the years I have always thought of it as Georgian, and it may be, but its windows are Victorian.

Next was the grocers and sweet shop of Mr F. Curle. All the children of the village enjoyed many a halfpenny's worth of his sweet dust and hard jubes.

His shop had an overhang across its front which was very handy for the village boys to congregate under after dark, especially on Guy Fawkes night, when they would throw their fireworks and squibs at any girls wanting to pass, so it was a case of running the gauntlet against the squibs. Still, it was fun.

Next door was a bakery and shop owned and run by Mr Chisnell, the baker. Later came Mr Amos, and Mr Isom was the last occupant as a baker. What a huge oven it was where they baked the bread and so dark when you looked inside, until the baker lit his little Aladdin's lamp and placed it on a long-handled splat, opening the oven door to push it in the oven when he started to get the bread out, placing the lovely smelling loaves on top of the huge flour troughs. It was then time for the people to bring their dinners for baking. What a variety of menus — it is a wonder how the baker placed them all, cooked to perfection too; crust around the dish with pigsticken; yorkshire pudding with meat in the centre; rice puddings; meat pies; etc, ready for people to call for them about a quarter to one. It has always remained a mystery to me how the bakers were able to bake so many different dishes perfectly. I never heard of any dinner spoilt in the baking.

Rowhedge Ferry about 1904. Mr Talbot, the ferryman, in bowler hat. Captain Alfonso Lay of the big steam yacht *Vanadis*, in plain clothes, stands in the flat bottomed ferryboat. A cruising yachts fits out against Pearson's Quay (left) with Chisnell's bakery behind. The house of the Jones family and Mr Heath's coal shed are in centre, then the *Ship Hotel* and the house of Mr Cooper, the yachting tailor. The church and school visible in the background. Yacht hands stand on the ferry hard, where a yacht's cutter lies.

After all the dinners had been called for, Mr Ladbrook (Mr Chisnell's son-in-law) set to and delivered the bread to houses in the village by hand cart. I believe at that time a quartern cost 2½ old pence. Eventually Mr Chisnell had a new house, bakery and shop built which he named the Coronation Bakery, 1902. It still stands today, situated at the top of Albion Street, no longer a bakery but a nursing home, renamed Albion House.

Returning to the High Street and to the bakery which Mr Chisnell had now left: it was opened as a sweet shop for a time by Mr F. Howe. There was once a fire in the shop and I remember seeing the charred remains of its contents. Whether it spread to other parts of the building I cannot say, but it eventually became a bakery again carried on by Mr E. Amos and one of his sons. After several years they moved further up the street, where there was another house and bakery more or less adjoining Stacey Woods grocery shop, at one time run by Mr Pitt.

We now retrace our steps to the Post Office Lane which was next to Chisnells. Here several cottages were tucked away, one was lived in only for a short time by two "peculiar persons" because they probably occupied a derelict one. They were "Gooseberry Lil" and "Captain Splasher", counterparts of the district's most noted tramps, "Marmalade Emma and Grimes". Their stay in Rowhedge, if one could call it a stay, was very brief indeed, but I can remember them setting out on their wanderings, complete with an old pram; "Gooseberry Lil" pushing it and talking to herself all the time and "Captain Splasher" in his old overcoat, bedraggled and dirty, as they both were, he always trailing behind. I suppose that was how they existed, going from village to village in the Colchester area; peculiar people indeed.

We are now back in High Street and about to pass Ferry Cottage where Mrs Jones, owner of the Rowhedge ferry, was living with her children; a very nice family indeed, who hailed, I believe, from Wivenhoe. Just before the First World War they moved to Ferry House and Mr Christopher Jones lived there until recently.

Next to the ferry cottage was the large black coal shed belonging to Mr Jim Heath, the coal merchant of Wivenhoe. His main coal depot was on the Wivenhoe marshes near the toll gate and the railway sidings and quay, and when the tide was very low he, or one of his men, would load up their coal cart and bring the coal to Rowhedge by horse and cart, fording the river at the ferry. From time to time they would stock up the coal shed and then sell it to customers in Rowhedge. The coal shed is now garages opening on to the grassy space which is the forecourt of what was then the *Ship Hotel*, now a private house. Sometimes men known as "cheap jacks" would come to the forecourt and ply their wares, which were mostly kitchen utensils and crockery.

At the north side of the forecourt stood Ferry House, the name it has today, where Mr Cooper and his family lived. He was the men's tailor of the village and practically all his working time was spent in making new suits for many of the yachts' crews that sailed from Rowhedge. When a yacht fitted out in the spring each member of her crew was provided with one new navy blue suit, reefer jacket style, two pairs of blue trousers, two blue or white jerseys with the yacht's name embroidered across the chest and the initials of the yacht club below, a cheesecutter cap with two cap covers, one sun hat, one pair of canvas deck shoes, one pair of black leather shoes and one oilskin coat and sou-wester hat. This was a basic outfit of clothes for a hand. Mates and captains, stewards and engineers of course had more and different clothing, all paid for by the yacht owner, who wished his crew to look as smart as possible. Some yachts, particularly racers and larger craft, had their own colour-striped stocking caps too and white duck suits, like boiler suits.

The village shoemakers, Mr Alf Everitt and Mr Southgate, handmade the shoes and also supplied the white canvas deck shoes. These two men were "masters of their craft" each working in his own premises.

The smart crews, scrubbed white decks, polished brass and white sails, made a pretty scene. I was reminded of this when summer holidaying at Cowes recently; a very large yacht came in painted white, with white sails and the eleven men on the deck were in white duck trousers, scarlet jerseys and stocking caps; it was wonderful to see it again as it was years ago, always a beautiful sight on a sunny day.

Now we have arrived at the ferry hard, where the ferry boat plied across the river to the Wivenhoe bank. We must linger for awhile, for it was here that the sailormen would congregate, spin their yarns, take a look at the weather and state of tide; this was where all the gossip and news of the village was discussed and turned over. Some of the men would stand and talk in groups, others walked up and down as they talked, viewing everyone as they passed by, until at last the pubs opened. Many went in them for a drink, the favourite term for that being "half a shoot", meaning a half pint, and many consumed more than the half shoot, which was their affair, after all.

There were two more such walks in the High Street, one on the Albion Quay, the other on the Lion Quay. It was always said that the captains and mates of the yachts walked the Albion Quay and Lion Quay and their crews walked the ferry hard. Usually they paced up and down in a little line as they talked, hands behind backs, intent on the conversation, but always taking only a certain number of steps and then all turning together, without any sort of signal, and pacing an equal number of steps back, like walking a deck. During their talk they gave way to no one, intent on the discussion, but I am sorry to say that eventually this custom died out as the years went by. It was part of a way of life, and with it went the sailormen too and by 1973 there are only three men left in the village who have spent practically their whole working lives at sea; they are—Messrs Fred Mills, Jess Carter and Henry Cook.*

*Regrettably all have since passed on.

Going down Church Lane, as I do very often to do my little shopping, one arrives automatically at the ferry hard. I recall thoughts of long ago as I often look around and remember, and view the state of the tide and prospects of the weather for the day. The activities around the ferry hard are now but memories of a way of life which linger in some people's minds as they do in mine. As I was passing this spot recently I turned and said to one of the last surviving sailormen of the village, "Where are they now?" "Gone," he replied. "Well," I said, "if there aren't any ghosts walking here, I'll be surprised." He laughed and we both went on our way.

Now we will wander on up High Street and pass the entrance to Church Lane, much wider today than in earlier times, before Mrs Dove's house, which was attached to the present Post Office, was demolished. When passing it to go up Church Lane as a child, I thought of it as a sombre-looking place. The front had only one downstair window, the roof practically came down to the top of this, and out of it jutted a dormer window. The house was black-tarred all over, but the curtains were always snow white, and Mrs Dove was very old, with snow white hair and always dressed in black. As most of the side of the house was ivy clad, boys would keep her busy, asking "Please Mrs Dove can we try (shake) your ivy", and her answer would be "No, that you shan't boy!" Mrs Dove's ivy was the first port of call for the boys when setting out at night to go up to the heath bird catching. They could often be seen going up the street with their stock in trade of this escapade, carrying with them nets on two poles bent over at the top, and lanterns which when lit they would shine on the bushes, where they hoped the poor little birds would be. Then, bang on the bush went the nets, and the birds, if any, would fall into the pocket which went across the whole width of the net. Then they would kill them and put them into the bags they carried. But they didn't kill the linnets and would never kill a robin, so a man told me last year who used to go bird catching himself. There were, I've no doubt, many sparrow pies eaten in Rowhedge years ago. I remember eating bird pie but that particular one wasn't sparrow pie, as the birds were larger so I suppose they were either blackbirds or thrushes and when one comes to think of it, what a shame it was to kill those little birds. But it was always done and my brothers William and Jack went too, for it had gone on in Rowhedge for many, many years before. Now there are no bird catching adventures for it died out completely long ago, and I don't think it would be allowed today.

In theory, we are still outside the front of Mrs Dove's house and pass on to the shop next door which was a haberdashers and toy shop owned by Mrs F. Curle. It did quite good business in the village, selling all the usual materials for making underclothing, Calico at 3¾d per yard, madopalan* perhaps 1d dearer, and nainsook† too. She stocked all kinds of prints, and as the women of Rowhedge were good needle workers in those days they found Mrs Curle's

*a material.
†a kind of muslin.

shop very handy. Men's shirts, socks and underwear were found there, and she specialized in children's pinafores, some nicely embroidered or lace-flounced, the best ones with a pink or blue ribbon bow on the left of the chest, and practically every one was white. Girls used to go to school in pinafores over their dresses in my young days, and we all took a pride in them and tried to keep them looking nice and clean, as the mothers had more than their share of starching and ironing with no electric irons to lighten the burden, only hot flats or box irons. Before gas came to Rowhedge, about 1913, all the heat for the irons had come from the coal fire. Children wore pinafores at home too and certainly never ate a meal without one on. One remembers that at dinner on Sundays, especially in summer time, we always changed from our Sunday dresses to an everyday one and, if the weather was favourable, we would sit down to our dinner in just our petticoats and pinafore. Clothes had to be treated with great care as they had to last as long as possible, but every child I feel sure had Sunday and week-day clothes, and the women had the same. So Mrs Curle sold her pinafores and sundries and she employed two assistants, one mostly on the toy counter and the other on the drapery counter. I would never have wanted to serve in that shop because it always seemed so melancholy to my young mind, but my word on Christmas Eve it really did wake up. The shop would be bodily full of shoppers and quite a trade was done, and the white pinafores were in great demand. You might say when reading this "why wait until Christmas Eve and cause the rush to buy?" Well, I'm afraid that wasn't always from choice as money in Rowhedge was far from plentiful, especially in mid-winter when more money was needed for coal and light, for instance. I don't know what a tradesmen's money was in the shipyard in those times but I do know that the wages of "lumpers" (what labourers were then called) were 18/- per week, and I have been told that shipwright's pay was 30/-. As for the hands that went on the smacks spratting, well if the catch at the end of each week was poor, perhaps that would mean for the crew only a few shillings. At "stowboating", as spratting was called, five shares in money had to come out of the catch; one share for the boat, one share for the owner, and one share each for the crew which consisted of three men. So such situations made it impossible for many to buy these little presents until around Christmas Eve, when the shop eventually closed at 11 p.m. In earlier times this shop was occupied by the Glozier family before they moved to Wivenhoe. The building is three storied and the top floor was a sail maker's loft at one time owned by a Mr Pattison.

Taking you up this High Street slowly, we will move only a few paces to what until recent years was the Post Office. The then post master was Mr Tom Pitt. I can still clearly remember both him and his wife. He was a church warden and on Sunday nights after the collection had been taken, he would leave his pew, walk up the aisle and get back to the Post Office in time to seal the mail bag, which Harry Fairweather, the postman, would be waiting to take over the ferry to Wivenhoe Station to be placed on the train for London.

Next we come to the home of Mr Wakeland who had his boot repairing shop in his front garden. Mr and Mrs Wakeland were both very quiet, sincere people with a family of five sons and one daughter named Flo. She was well liked by all the girls of the village and everyone's friend. We who knew her were all sorry at her recent passing.

Now we have arrived at the *White Lion*, in its day quite a distinctive building, as it still is, but no longer a public house, only private houses. We will walk on, past the entrance to Regent Street so as to arrive at Stacey's Corner and Stacey Woods' grocery shop, where Mr John Watsham was the manager and was fair and courteous to one and all. The goods for stocking-up came from Wivenhoe, via the ferry. Stacey Woods came to Rowhedge from Mersea, and after he was established in Rowhedge, he moved over to Wivenhoe and also opened a grocery shop there. Yet in Rowhedge, Stacey's Corner is still there, but few remember it as such. It was the boys' equivalent of the ferry hard, where many would gather to air their views, argue and squabble, and watch the smacks and boats, yachts and sailing barges going up and down river.

Next we arrive at Mr Crosby's shop, but I was too young to remember him being the occupant. Charles Powell came later, the oldest son of Captain Isiah Powell, captain of Lord Brassey's famous yacht the *Sunbeam*. I remember a fire that broke out at the shop and the charred remains of part of the front of it. My family lived only two doors away and we were all terribly anxious that the fire would spread to the row of cottages where I lived, with their backs mostly of timber, as was Powell's shop. However it was got under control, and we were able to go home and sleep in peace.

The Essex earthquake of 22nd April, 1884, nearly did its worst for Mr Crosby's house and shop as the photo, which includes the Crosby family, clearly shows. For all that the earthquake did to the property, it still stands today and is still a shop, but its yard is now a garage and repair yard. The earthquake evidently caused some peculiar incidents at Rowhedge. The late Mr Edward Crickmore remembered being in the infants' class at the school that day and a man was shaken off a ladder while repairing the clock. It was also said that a baby in the village smothered while its mother ran out in alarm as the tiles crashed off the house roof and the walls trembled.

Another step or two and we are at a row of cottages where my family lived and where I was born. In the photo of them you can only see our front windows and garret, but not the front door; it was evidently taken at such an angle that one cannot see the first cottage at all. Also in the photo are four young children, including the late Reg Knights, with the milk cart and the milkman, Mr Gerry Woods. He came to his customers each day from Fingringhoe and sold his milk in halfpennies and pennies worth. I remember him as a very nice type of man, always tidy in himself and with a pleasant word for everyone whether they bought off him or not. Many went to the farms for milk; it must have been cheaper that way. Some children went as far as to the middle of Page's Chase at Fingringhoe, to Rowland Taylor's Farm to buy milk, and before breakfast too. My brother George told me he also used to go, quite a walk so early in the morning unless they cycled, which I doubt. I occasionally went to Donyland Hall for milk when Mr Robinson farmed there and later Mr Miller, a Scotsman, but we girls went more often to Battleswick Farm, after the Robinson family moved there. Here, when the kitchen door opened, we could have a good look into the room. It had a huge fireplace in it and a copper by the side of it nearly as big as the fireplace, and some kind of a sink with a large water pump standing over it. One cupboard I remember was

Looking up the upper end of High Street. Crosby's shop at extreme left. Our house immediately beyond. Mr Jerry Woods and his milk cart in the street and children wearing pinafores. The little boy in straw hat at left is the late Mr Reg Knights. Houston's shipyard "big shed" in right background.

HIGH STREET
ROWHEDGE. No 13

Crosby's (later Fales') shop in the High Street, after the Essex earthquake in 1884, with the Crosby family standing outside. The shop still stands.

nearly as big as the kitchens of years ago and the door latches at Battleswick were made of wood. Sometimes we would get to the farm too early, before the milk had cooled sufficiently, so we would go into the farmyard to watch the cows being milked, see the pigs and piglets in their styes and then to the ducks on the pond. We would go back to the dairy when we thought the milk would be ready and after having our cans filled, we lost no time in getting home as we couldn't bowl our hoops on the return journey.

We must now return to the High Street. After passing three other houses (long since demolished) we come to Dark House Lane; why so strange a name? I cannot enlighten you on that but five brick-built houses still remain, three others being demolished long ago. There were also several wooden houses and in one of these lived a very bent old lady named Mary Ann Di-Bart Shave. I have often thought I would like to have known more about her; and whether she was the owner of those wooden houses. I know that the property was sold prior to the First World War and Mr E Goodrum bought it. Later it was sold to the Colchester Manufacturing Company who established a clothing factory there.

So back down Dark House Lane we will come and to the Shipyard House. Quite a large house it was too, and I have often wondered if whether in more prosperous days Mary Ann Shave lived there, because the late Mr James Theobald said that the big shipyard shed now stands on what was once Mary Ann Shave's flower garden, so who knows. I won't linger around the shipyard as my son John has already written on its rise and decline in his book *The Northseamen* but we will pass on to *The Three Crowns*, a public house until a few years back. It is spoken of as the oldest house in Rowhedge, and maybe the dampest after it had stood empty for about a year. However, I think it has been purchased quite recently, and if restored can become a very attractive property. I have no idea of its age, but as the north-west side of it is definitely the older part, my guess is that it is well over four hundred years old and may be older. Now we are at the top of the street, where once stood four cottages. The one at the top end was occupied for a time by a native of Rowhedge named Mr William Warren. He had spent most of his life away from the village, being a gentleman's valet. However, he eventually settled in Rowhedge again and set up a dried fish shop in the front room of his cottage, selling mostly kippers and bloaters. On certain days he could be seen with a flat bottomed basket, calling on customers at their houses, plying his fish. At one house the occupant usually liked some bloaters and when he knocked at the door and it was opened Mr Warren, always polite, said, "Any bloaters today, Ma'am? Large as whales, Ma'am!". When she said that she couldn't buy any that day his reply was, "Oh, I can trust you, Ma'am, goodday". He eventually moved from the cottage when he married and went to live at The Glebe.

Now we have arrived at the top of High Street and must cross to its other side to see the waterside in the next chapter.

CHAPTER TWO

Downstreet

O N THE river side of the High Street, at its upper end opposite Head Street, is the Marsh Stile Gate, another place where boys of the village used to congregate. Its name indicates that it is the entrance to the up-street marshes and river wall which stretches away towards Colchester Hythe; a good vantage point for seeing anyone coming along the wall. Very often in spring and summer, late in afternoon or early evening, a short, middle-aged man might be seen coming towards Rowhedge. Someone would spot him and say, "Here comes old Zike", the bird catcher with his basket, on his way to the Pightle* and the green bank of the lower gardens of Donyland Hall, via the willows' path by the Roman river. This was a favourite spot for gold finches and grey linnets, so I suppose each time he visited there he took toll of these two beautiful songsters. So much for Old Zike; he would come and go, doing harm to no one except the birds.

Before I leave the Marsh Stile Gate, which I must say is unrecognisable as a gate today, there was another such traveller who came along the wall to Rowhedge, but he was in quite another line of business from Zike. This man was always known as "Pincushion". He would trundle to Rowhedge pushing his three-wheeled contraption of a handcart and trying to sell — of all things — paraffin oil. Who his customers were I do not know, but some people must have bought from him as he came to Rowhedge quite regularly and on Saturday afternoons he would return to sell his basket full of watercress. But what he endured from the boys while trying to sell his wares must have tried his patience, although I know he looked a funny old man and was always mumbling to himself. One of their favourite annoyances was to follow him along the streets shouting out "Pincushion nicked the baby". What this meant I have never found out but it seemed senseless to me. As he went from house to house with his wares, the boys would quickly tie up the wheels of his chariot, and there would be Pincushion mumbling and fumbling, trying to get the wheels free. Poor old chap, he certainly did have a lot to put up with, but the boys evidently thought it was great sport — naughty boys maybe, but boys will be boys, it is said, whether in the tenth or the twentieth century. All this happened in my early school days, but there came a time when Pincushion came no more and maybe at last he had found his rest.

In winter, many yachts lay on the mud along the river wall above the village and here, just above the shipyard, lay two big old smacks; the *Concord*,

*A word which signified a small enclosure.

35

owned by Mr Ambrose Walford and the *Industry* by William White. I can remember their ageing owners occasionally going on board but eventually the smacks were broken up for firewood.

Our return journey is down the river side of the High Street, passing a row of houses which backed on to the shipyard and ended adjoining its main gate. On the other side of this was Mr Cole's pork butcher's shop, kept scrupulously clean and tidy, where he sold pork, pork cheese and chitlins. He lived in the house almost adjoining the shop and next to the workers' entrance to the shipyard.

At 6.30 a.m. each morning we heard the shipyard bell, the time when men then started their daily work. A hurried shuffle of many feet was often heard up the street before the bell stopped ringing, for if by then they had not got in the shipyard gate, they had to "lose a quarter", which meant a quarter of an hour's pay. The shipyard, owned by Mr John Houston, built wooden craft of various kinds, besides hauling up many yachts, large and small, on its slipway to be repaired and refitted. Sometimes smacks were dealt with and I remember our *Beatrice* going on the slip to have a new deck. It was a busy, noisy place with hammering and sawing and the bright fires of the blacksmith's shop flickering and the ring of an anvil. Sometimes there were flags flying and cheers for the launching of a new yacht or other craft. Its previous owner had been a Mrs Puxley; perhaps strange for a woman to own a shipyard, although I believe she inherited it from her husband. Anyway it had earlier been known as Puxleys Yard and I believe before that it was called Cheeks.

We now pass the "big shed" where so many wooden craft were built, including a large number of R.N.L.I. lifeboats. What a joy they were to behold with craftsmanship evident even to the eyes of little children, their paintwork shone so vividly in their bright colours. Beyond this was an opening to a quayside, at the front of which my Uncle Dick Cranfield and Mr Alf Everitt lived in two very nice semi-detached houses. Uncle Dick was a yacht skipper and owned the fine smack *Ellen*. I was always welcome at my Uncle Dick's home and as they had a piano I often went there, for from my earliest memories, hearing a piano being played really enchanted me, as indeed to this very day it still does. My cousin Emmie Cranfield was a very accomplished pianist, and as I sat in the room when she was playing it was absolute bliss to my ears. There came a time, at least for a few years, that they had two pianos in the room. The small one was a yacht's piano, brought ashore and indoors for the winter months, and I was sometimes allowed to try with care to play a few notes on it, which was wonderful to my little mind.

Mr Owers and family occupied the next house and sweet shop. It was a pleasant and roomy house which also had two stables at the back. On one side it had a large loft under which a cart could be kept. Next was another quay, Webbers Quay. Two good houses stood on part of it; Captain Alf Cranfield

Looking down the High Street from outside the "big shed" of Houston's shipyard. I was born in the house in the centre of the picture, visible immediately beyond the narrow wooden house (right).

and Mr Allen and their respective families lived there at that time. These houses were almost always partially flooded at very high tides, and as the rows of houses that I lived in were directly opposite this quay, water sometimes lapped our back door steps too. Strange as it may seem, it never threatened the front ways but came up the drains at the back of the houses. We often hear today that a flood warning has gone out, but it is no different today from those years ago, where at very high tides it could be expected, and indeed would rush in places over the marsh walls, both up-street and down-street, flooding the marshes. On one such occasion I remember the high tide together with the fury of the waves caused quite a lot of anxiety. The smacks at the quays were riding it out very high, huge gashes were made in the sea walls and it flooded the marshes deeply. Very cold and frosty weather followed and it became a lovely skating rink for those who could skate. I wasn't one of them, I can assure you, but I can recall one boy in particular, Harold Burch from Albion Street, who was remarkable on the ice. For a time after he left school he sailed as a boy on my father's smack the *Beatrice*. I can still picture him down in the little cabin aft, about to have his tea before they went down the river; his basket with his food in it, butter I remember being in a small platter container, and his bread and jam. Later on he went deep-sea and made it his life's career, eventually becoming master of a large merchant ship. He sailed mostly from America and it was there that he married a young American lady, and both his father and mother went to America to be present at his wedding. When he retired he came back to England to spend his halcyon days, living in Colchester. He bought a yacht and kept it at the lower yard, Rowhedge, and with his family spent many happy days sailing around the Colne and Blackwater.

I must return to Webbers Quay where several smacks were moored. The *Ellen* CK 222, owner Mr Henry Martin, next to my father's *Beatrice* CK 156. I am not sure whether the *Xanthe*, Captain W. Cranfield's smack, laid there or on the outside of the *Sunbeam* at the Lion Quay. This Mr W. Cranfield was also captain of the yacht *Xanthe*, owned by a judge, Mr Justice Channel. At the further end of the quay, immediately in front of two cottages, laid the smack *Four Sisters* owned by Davy Martin. He was getting too old to walk the plank to get aboard his craft, so he had to crawl. The smack, *Swedenborg*, owned by Mr Cheek, lay there too. She was strangely named after the religious group whose prophet was a Swede and who worshipped at the Swedenborg Church in Wivenhoe.

Webbers Quay in autumn 1908. My father's smack *Beatrice* CK 156 lies fitting out for winter fishing on the extreme right. The white yacht in centre is the *Chula*, built at John Houston's yard and captained by my uncle, Richard Cranfield. The black yacht beyond is the *Xanthe*. In the background a sailing barge with mast lowered is towed upriver by trace horse.

The smack *Xanthe,* owned by Captain W. Cranfield. He was no relation to the owner of the smack *Sunbeam*, Captain William W. Cranfield.

My father collected the dues for any moorings at this quay and as a little girl I would walk up to Old Heath with him to pay the moneys in to Mrs Webber, the owner. She lived in a large Victorian house named Victory House in the road now known as Fingringhoe Road. When my father and I rang the front door bell, the maid would open it and when Mrs Webber was told who we were, she would stand in the hall to welcome us. She was quite a lady, for those days, dressed always in black and on her head she wore a very dainty pale cream lace cap, threaded with very narrow black velvet—yes, typically Victorian, both in dress and poise. However, for all that, we would be invited into what I suppose was the drawing-room, where we were given light refreshment, and then taken for a walk around the gardens. With a basket of apples and pears to bring home, we would take our leave and offer our thanks. Victory House was demolished about 1968 and a block of flats is now built on the site.

Many ketch barges such as this one brought cargoes of coal to Crosby's Quay from the north-east coast ports. The *Hesper, Alice Watts* and beautifully named *Startled Fawn* were regular traders.

Now as we walk a few steps we arrive at Crosby's Quay which adjoined Webbers. The Crosbys traded in coal which was then brought to Rowhedge by ketch barges, a much larger type of vessel than the smacks, and in earlier days square-rigged brigs and barquentines also brought coal from the north east coast. I have seen a photograph of a square-rigged vessel and a steam boat, alongside Crosby's Quay, which amazed me, but certainly proved a point, that square-riggers as well as the ketch barges did deliver coal to Crosby's. The coal, when unloaded, was stacked in the large black shed on the quay and then sold in the village and beyond.

The Crosbys had owned a very large smack with two masts, a ketch named *New Blossom* which had evidently been built for fishing or to carry coal and sometimes other cargoes, but by then she was a hulk lying on the hard at No Man's Land played on by children until she was broken up.

Now we have come to No Man's Land which stretched from the boundary of Crosby's to where the Lion Quay began, a few feet to the south of the *White Lion Hotel* boundary. The smacks *Varuna, First Fruits* and *Mary* often lay there. On early mornings when the tide was high there were often smacks' boats bobbing there at the water's edge while the boys ran to Mr Pitt's nearby bakery to get the supplies of bread for their smack — large quartern loaves, cottage style in shape — scuttling off with them before the smack hoisted sail and glided swiftly downstream and to sea on the ebb.

This piece of land and waterside, once known as Bakers Hard, has been the cause of endless controversy for many years, and is still. While the firm of Cox and King were in the shipbuilding industry around 1902 at Rowhedge top yard, they evidently intended to incorporate No Man's Land into their firm, which led to what today would be called a "show down". Cox and King's workmen were told to take the wood and their tools to erect a fence across the whole of No Man's Land waterfront, and of course they had to obey, but no sooner had they started than word got around as to what was going on, and many men of the village, then home from sea, rushed to the scene and pulled down the fence as fast as the shipyard workers tried to erect it because they were determined to keep it as free mooring and access to one and all. In the end the shipyard men had to give it up, and for many years it remained No Man's Land, with anchorage free for any villager to keep a boat there. Writing of this particular spot does recall one tragedy, when Mr Tom Jay junior's young son lost control of his bicycle going down Regent Street, crossed the High Street, plunged into the river at No Man's Land and was drowned.

Next we come to the Lion Quay where many smacks would lie; the big old *Druid* next to Mr James Simons' *Hildegarde* and Uncle William Cranfield's swift *Sunbeam* by the *Foxhound*, owned by Mr Goodwin. On the quay itself a small fair, of all things, would at some time occupy it for a few days almost every year. It consisted of one set of swinging boats, a coconut shy stall, rock stall, and what one could term a small shooting gallery, where one could see small balls bobbing up and down when shooting was in progress. That was the lot. A Mrs Rose was the proprietor and oh, what a voice she had! It could be heard half way down the street with her shout of "Roll up, Roll up!". There came a time when, like Pincushion, she came no more, and no one heaved a sigh I'm sure.

A row of houses stood on the Lion Quay, backing on to *The Anchor* public house.

The large smack *Aquiline*, owned by Captain Harry Cook, lay at the Anchor Quay. She flew a black flag with a white gamecock in the centre at her tall topmasthead and on Sundays and holidays she also flew a large blue pennant with a yellow scalloped edge and a white letter A in the centre of it. The *Aquiline* was the last of the very large smacks to sail from Rowhedge and she was sold away during the First World War.

Now we are at *The Anchor* public house, the scene of many hectic times inside and out in those far off days. I remember one such an occasion, at Christmastime, although I never witnessed it. It was one Boxing Day, well past dinner time. Our smack, the *Beatrice*, had had a poor catch the previous week so my brother Jim, her skipper at the time, thought it a good idea to set out on the late afternoon tide to go down the river spratting; that was of course if he could get his crew in the mind to do so. He evidently tried to find them and someone told him that they were in *The Anchor*. So my brother put his suggestion to them there, they followed him out, and the next moment he received terrible punches in the face and was knocked about. His nose evidently took the full weight of the punching for the scar remained with him till the end of his days; and this he received from one of his own first cousins, no less. I suppose the *Beatrice* changed crews after that, and I don't think my brother ever forgot that experience, he always being a sober and thrifty man.

Here we are back at the ferry hard, the pivot of the village where men walked and talked as I have mentioned earlier and also where fights sometimes occurred late at night. Probably endless tales could be told of them but I know of none because my own family were never interested in that way of life.

Now that we are down by the ferry perhaps it is as well to stay there for awhile and remember how clean it was in those days, for each time the ferryman had a fare, before leaving either side of the river he would wash down part of the hard with a bailer as the tide was leaving it, to prevent muddy shoes when one stepped from the ferryboat. These boats, of which there were two, were extremely good weather boats, in spite of their being flat bottomed. I believe they carried 16 persons officially, but when the men from Rowhedge and Wivenhoe shipyards came to and fro in them, the figure was much higher, but for all that I have never heard of any mishap, either to the boats or passengers, and people were always taken across, come wind come weather. This was confirmed by the late Mr James Theobald, who used the ferry for many years on his way back and forth to Wivenhoe shipyard. There was one occasion when I thought I might be in trouble when crossing. One Saturday I had spent the day with my brother George and his family who lived on Wivenhoe Cross, and he was bringing me home to Rowhedge, after tea. It was dark, frosty and snowing, and the river had more than its share of ice floes. However, the ferry boat struggled across, in we stepped and then it all began. The tide must have been running in fast, and we got in a pack of ice floes. In spite of all that the ferryman and my brother were trying to do to get the boat's head round, we found ourselves going up the river and it was only just before we got near the first "bridge" that her head did come round, and with difficulty we eventually arrived at the ferry hard at Rowhedge. I was of course very scared all the time, being only about eight years old, only comforted because I was with my brother who was a powerful swimmer, and I knew that if anything happened he would do all he could to save me. Nothing did happen and we reached dry land safely, but I had been so frightened that I have never forgotten.

Now in a happier vein I will tell of the days in summer when the sun shone and all the world seemed bright; how the children would go to the hard to paddle, when the tide was right of course, and in between the time that it took for the ferry boat to get to the Wivenhoe side and back, the children had high jinks paddling and splashing one another, but often the ferryman would more than frown on them if ever they got in his way. Looking across the river from the Rowhedge side one could often see the trace horse and its horseman on their way from the Hythe to the railway quay at Wivenhoe to pick up a sailing barge in a calm. With ropes thrown aboard, the horse and its rider would then pull the barge up to the Hythe. This was often done and I have seen it many many times, so when we, the inhabitants of Rowhedge and Wivenhoe, lost the right of way of the direct Wivenhoe wall about 1967 and were "offered" the river wall as an alternative, we were being given nothing, as this wall was not only a public wall but a bridle path too!

I recall the building of a huge corrugated shed on the Wivenhoe marsh, more or less opposite Rowhedge ferry. No one had any idea what such a building was being erected for and it was all hush hush for a long time, which gave rise to many rumours. However, eventually the secret came out—an aeroplane was being built there; then a very rare sight. The designer was a Mr

Mr Jack Humphrey's aerohydroplane ready to be launched on Wivenhoe marsh, opposite Rowhedge, in 1909. The machine is facing the camera. The pilot sat in the wooden chair just visible on the centre hull.

The aerohydroplane ready for take off on the Colne, off Beacon Wood. Mr. Humphrey in pilot seat. I am in one of the spectator rowboats in the background.

Jack Humphrey of Halstead. Local boat builders were employed in the building of it and no doubt Mr Humphrey took a hand in it too. I have been told that the engine was 35 horse power and drove two propellers which were mounted behind the pilot, who sat on a chair. It looked a peculiar contraption of wings and wires and on completion was called an "aerohydroplane" as it took off from the water on floats, the word seaplane not yet in use. I remember quite well going over on to the Wivenhoe bank at the ferry and seeing it brought to the water's edge. It went in head first. I suppose Mr Humphrey was by that time in his seat and had to scramble out. The seaplane was soon hauled out of the water and taken back to its hangar. After a while it reappeared again, this time to go down the river off Beacon Wood, near Alresford Creek, where the Colne is much wider, with Mr Humphrey hoping for success on this attempt. It was towed down to Beacon Wood, there being no other means of getting it there, where a great number of people in rowing boats were awaiting its arrival (I was one of them) and to see it take off. Again it was failure for it never lifted itself at all. So it was back to Wivenhoe marsh for the plane and home for the onlookers in the rowing boats.

Not to be daunted Mr Humphreys altered the plane to attempt to win a prize of £1,000 offered by the *Daily Mail* newspaper for the first Briton to fly over a mile. He fitted it with wheels to take off from land and evidently put in a bigger engine of 60 horse power. That October it was brought out of the shed on the marsh and again Mr Humphrey climbed into the seat to cheers from the crowd. The aeroplane ran ahead fast but fell into a ditch, smashing the propellers and its underparts.

Mr Humphrey still had faith in the aeroplane and during November he tried to fly from a field near Berechurch Road, but again was unsuccessful. A few days later he had another go on the cavalry training ground, but after that he gave up. All this happened in the year 1909, and after this the plane was broken up and its seaplane floats came to rest under the moulding loft of the lower yard of Rowhedge Ironworks. There is one photo of it as an aeroplane, taken on the marsh opposite Rowhedge and another photo taken off Beacon Wood when it was a seaplane. A very disappointed Mr Humphrey failed to see his dreams come true.

Another strange thing built at Wivenhoe was a small submarine named *Volta*. Although I do not remember seeing this it was talked of often and I believe was built in 1905 at the shipyard of Forrestt and Son, in great secrecy. I have read that she was thirty-four feet long, was driven by an electric motor and had a crew of three men. As there was war between Russia and Japan at the time, the submarine evidently caused quite a stir, but I believe was owned by a firm and was not part of our Navy. No one seems to know what happened to her.

We cannot leave the ferry scene, or at least I can't, without comment on the corrugated iron hut which served as the ferry shelter on the Wivenhoe

Making a sail on the quay, about 1919. Mr Elisha Wade of the *William Henry* (seated) talks to George Cranfield (left) and Mr Clarke (right). The corrugated iron ferry shelter on the Wivenhoe bank in the background.

bank from my earliest days. It still stands (1972), bashed about quite a bit maybe, but still in one piece. It was even moved about three years ago from its original site, about thirty feet to the south — a remarkable advertisement for corrugated iron!

Today we miss the pleasant scene looking across the river where, until very recent years, we could see cattle grazing on the marshes, sometimes standing practically at the water's edge. But now the scene has changed and we can see only huge stacks of timber, and as time goes by there will be more of them, I have no doubt.

Sailing barges passing up the river to the Hythe were an everyday sight. Most sailed, others were poled, towed or taken by trace horse, according to tide, wind and weather. Sailing ships came up river to Wivenhoe and laid on buoys there, to unload timber into lighters which were poled up to the Hythe at Colchester and the timber wharves. Then only two steam boats used the river; the *Gem* and the *Eager*. I believe theirs was a cargo of coal bound for the gas works, but the barges carried all kinds of cargo, many to Marriages' Flour Mill with corn, others to Parry's oil mills with peanuts. On the return journeys some would sail with their decks stacked high with straw, so called the "stacky" barges.

Sailing barges like this brought cargoes of barley and barrels to the village brewery; heavily loaded yet sailed by two men.

Large numbers of sailing barges regularly traded into and out of the river.

The steam yacht *Gwendoline*, Captain Henry Sebborn, on the gridiron at Harris Brothers yard, about 1905. Part of Cat Island quay at left.

Smacks were placed on the ferry hard to have their bottoms scrubbed and be repainted or tarred, and many smacks' rowboats were kept there, when these were not in use.

Now we make our last stop in the High Street, at Pearson's Quay and those below it. Several smacks lay against Pearson's including Mr James Carter's *Wonder*, which was known as the "lucky" *Wonder* because of her good catches, the small smack *Jemima*, owned by Mr Tom Allen also lay there and sometimes the *Foxhound* owned by Mr Goodwin. Further down the quay, near *The Albion* public house, lay the *Neva* owned by Uncle Lemon Cranfield. She was the fastest smack of the village fleet and probably the fastest in Essex. He had been the most famous of racing yacht captains, winning scores of races in yachts of many sizes, from ten tonners to the very largest cutters and schooners. From the large sums of prize money he won at the helm of the cutter *Neva* he had Harris Yard build the smack *Neva* for him. She won first prize in the rowhedge and Wivenhoe regattas many times.

One year Lemon suggested to his brother William that they should secretly sail each other's smacks in the Rowhedge regatta. They changed places shortly before the start, down Colne. As the smacks came in sight below Rowhedge there was great excitement when it was seen that the *Sunbeam* was leading. But it was Uncle Lemon at the tiller, waving his cap and shouting "That had you. Thought the old man was beaten at last!".

Pearson's was one of the three quays where the stowboaters discharged when they were too late getting their catch into Brightlingsea to catch the fresh fish market, or to the railway quay at Wivenhoe. So when their luck was against them, the catch had to go for manure, and was sold at Pearson's Quay to Tom Pitt for 6d, and sometimes as low as 4d a bushel — all fresh fish. Many people of the village would go with their buckets to the heaps on the quays and help themselves to small whiting, pouts, dabs and sprats and all at no cost to themselves, and I cannot remember ever hearing of the fishermen being offered any money for them. So, precious little was the fishermen's lot out of it all, after toiling to catch them, then filling the bushel baskets and running them ashore. One of the crew had to stay on board at night until it was time to ease the masthead tackle, then it was home, perhaps for a short sleep and to sea on the next tide. According to the way the wind was blowing, it would be a beat against it all down the river, and so it went on.

These sprat heaps were re-sold to local farmers to be spread on their land. I remember the horses and tumbrils of James Pertwee of Langenhoe Hall would come for the bulk of them. Tragedy occurred at the quayside on one occasion, when two fine horses and a tumbril went over the quay at the southern-most end of it. I don't know why this happened as I didn't witness it, but I do remember most clearly looking over the quay near *The Albion* where I saw the drowned horses and tumbril lying in the mud.

My Uncle Richard Cranfield's smack *Ellen* lay off the Albion Quay and just beyond her, at a quay owned by Uncle Turner Barnard, lay the smacks *Violet*, another owned by Mr Zac Burch, the little *Unity* owned by Mr Daniel James, which had a square stern and was always called a "bawley", and the *Telegraph*, owned by Jack Cranfield, always known by his nickname of "Jack Pups". A good sailor and fisherman was he, with perhaps a touch of reckless dash in his make-up. I have heard it said that once, when a gale was blowing, he was anchored under the Colne beach, impatient because the weather kept him from fishing for days, like the fleet of Brightlingsea smacks anchored in the river. Eventually Jack's impatience overcame him and the others were astonished to see the *Telegraph* hoisting sail and going out of the river. They felt they couldn't let him put this one over on them so the whole fleet up-anchored and followed him, no doubt feeling very sore about being more or less forced to go out to fish in very rough conditions indeed. Jack Cranfield was a smart man in a racing yacht and had been mastheadsman in the America's Cup yachts, *Valkyrie II* and *III*.

Further down, my Uncle Stephen Cranfield's smack *Elizabeth Ann* lay alongside Arthur Cranfield's *Blanche* and the *Lily*, owned by Uncle Jonathan Cranfield, who lived opposite this quay, in Vine Cottage.

The *Elizabeth Ann* was once run into by the steamer *Essex* and sank in deep water. Stephen quickly sought the help of the other Rowhedge smacks *Neva* and *Wonder*, who sailed out to her and dragged big chains under the *Elizabeth Ann*, so that when the tide rose they lifted her up and brought her into shallow water to be repaired and eventually to sail again.

Like his brothers, Uncle John was captain of racing yachts and evidently had ordered the building of the *Lily* from Harris Yard before he sailed off one spring for the season's yachting. His brother Lemon Cranfield looked into the yard to see how the new smack was progressing and found they had just started. As he did not like the shape he told Mr Harris to take a foot off the beam (width) to make her faster, like the narrow racing yachts they had then. So, when Uncle John came home in the autumn, he found a new, lean smack awaiting him. I don't know if he was pleased or not!

At the end of them all, in a little dock to themselves, you would often find Mr Elisha Wade in his little bawley, the *William Henry*, the *Robert and Ann* of Captain Henry Sebborn and the small smack *Albion*, once named *Snowdrop* and owned by Uncle John O. Barnard, but by then sailed by Mr Brasted who kept *The Albion* public house. He used her in winter to dredge oysters on the Colne fishery and in summer, like many men from the village, he was in the crew of the King's racing yacht *Britannia*.

As we are at the brewery quay and Harris Yard, our journey up and down the High Street has ended and it is time to look at other things.

Captain John Carter and most of the crew of the royal racing cutter *Britannia* were from Rowhedge. She is seen here setting 10,000 square feet of sail and with a crew of thirty.

CHAPTER THREE

The Changing Year

BEFORE exploring more of the village, its people and events, I would like to recall something of the seasons of the year, starting with the spring, which brings us all new hope each year.

With the dark days of winter gone, signs of spring were everywhere apparent, coupled with a little sunshine; even the age-old east wind seemed to have lost some of its sting. Living in a seafaring family as I did, one soon learned to observe the times of the tides and the frolics of wind and weather. Most of my young life was spent living near the quay in a house that faced due east. It was one of four such houses, the backs of which must have been very old, there being a trap door in the ceiling of the kitchen of my home, which obviously had been the only way up to bed until, as I understand, new fronts, including a staircase, were built on to the houses at a later date.

Now come with me just across the street to the quays and see what we can find there. The large anchors from the fishing smacks had already been brought ashore together with the lee boards (fitted on the bulwarks) and stowboating gear that had been in use during the winter for the spratting season. For most of their crews it meant that the yachts were about to start fitting out, but some at least of the fishing smacks would soon be fitting out for the spring trawling season. Here we would also find Mr Alf Everitt busy in his shoemaker's shop so step inside, for there was always a welcome. Already his assistant, Mr Boyston from Fingringhoe, was there at his bench and that meant they were very busy. Rows of new hand-made shoes were in various stages of completion, from leather in the tub right up to the rows of shoes in their trees on shelves under the windows, waiting to be delivered to various yacht skippers for their crews. The shoes were all hand-made on the premises. Shoes were mended there which meant a welcome and a little chat.

Mr Everitt was a very genial and alert type of man and at odd times enjoyed a ride round the countryside in his pony and trap. He stabled his pony in the garden at the back of one of the houses where his aunt lived, and kept his hay in the loft which was over the kitchen. When he came to collect his pony one could hear its clippedy-clop over the bricks as it passed our door.

Mr Everitt, the shoemaker, at the reins of his pony and trap.

As the mornings grew lighter each day the village children were out and about much earlier, some to go to the brook at the bottom of Chapel Street with their pails for drinking water. Two steps led down to it and from time to time some child or other would "slump in" as we called it. Until a short time ago one could still see the steps, but now, more's the pity, they have gone. Of course the stream still flows under the road and through the marshes on its way to The Snuffy,* at the first "bridge" along the wall, and from there to the river. But now this access to the brook has been boarded up and I for one was sorry to see it go.

In those days many children went to the farms for milk before breakfast but no one seemed to be late for school. Both Battleswick Farm and Donyland Hall had their little callers. They served both new and twelve-houred milk; the twelve-houred being the cheaper was very popular and we got good measure.

*A marsh salt water drain leading through a culvert in the river wall to the river, by a rill in the mud.

They also sold skimmed milk. At Donyland Hall, where the Robinson family farmed, Miss Frances Robinson usually answered the dairy door and served us. One remembers her as a very regal figure and the gracious smiles she gave us helped us on our way.

Now we would go home and, after breakfast, start out for school. In early spring many school children played "join on" which consisted of the boys and girls forming a line and, taking hold of one another's coat tails, they would run up and down Church Lane, snake fashion, until the bell rang. After school, skipping ropes appeared and the aim was to skip in double ropes, which were usually pieces of rope from the yachts, given to them by their fathers. Of course, by this time the boys would be busy with their tops and whips and the bright colours that they had crayoned on the top made them look quite pretty. After skipping and tops the little season of the hoops came; wooden for the girls and iron for the boys and, as in those early days there was practically no traffic at all, we could all bowl our hoops up and down the street to our hearts' content.

By now pancake day had come and gone and children were looking forward to Easter. On Good Friday morning Mr Ladbrook would come round

Some of the Rowhedge schoolgirls. Myself at extreme left of third row from front. White pinafores were usual wear for school.

with hot cross buns, a halfpenny each, which he had made very early that morning at the bakery. Dinner that day for most of the inhabitants of Rowhedge meant fish, followed by rice pudding. Not rice pudding as we eat it today; far more rice was used in those days so that when it was cooked it could be cut in the dish and eaten either with a spoon or as one would eat a piece of cake, so solid was it. After such meal many children in separate little parties would go up to the heath and into the wood. No skipping ropes this time, for we went there to play hide and seek among the bushes, and when we found a tree with strong branches the boys, if there were any amongst us, would climb the tree and tie a rope to a branch to make a swing, for it was lovely to swing there and we would take it in turns. Others would go off looking for the "cuckoos" (wood anemones), the earliest flowers of spring in the heath and wood. The leaves of the bluebells had forced their way through the carpets of oak leaves, so in not too many weeks distant, bluebell land by the stream in the wood would be a blaze of beauty, and when that day came, walking towards them, a blue haze seemed to float over them. And there would be the primrose bank to be searched and wild violets too; how lovely they appeared in their pale shade of lavender. Primroses and wild violets still grow on the bank. After our frolics of the afternoon in the wood, we eventually made our way home, tired perhaps but happy. And soon it would be Easter Day. On the Saturday following Good Friday nearly everyone, I am sure, was given a new ball. Many had been covered by crocheting in wool; rainbow wool was most attractive. As for the boys, I am not sure what they did around Easter time, but I think many went up in the heath looking for birds' nests.

There was no organized sport in Rowhedge in those days, but I do remember boys played football on the marsh, though no real matches were played. Easter Day came and after having an egg for breakfast and receiving a little chocolate Easter egg, it would be time to get ready for Sunday School, which started for the Church of England children at 10 a.m. After the singing of hymns, prayers and a short reading from the Bible, we, with our teachers, walked in formation to the church for morning service which we attended once a month, and then after dinner, it was Sunday School again from 2.30 p.m. to 3.30 p.m. I assume that we did more or less the same on Easter Monday and on Good Friday, and after that we played with our skipping ropes until it was back to school again.

By this time, Rowhedge seemed to be quite a busy place. All the yachts, and there were a great many, were fitting out. One could see great activity on the quays, and along the "up street" wall where the yachts lay, the painters were busy; the spars on the "three corner" part of the marsh had had their winter covering taken off and were being rubbed down before varnishing. In the sunshine the linen lines in the various skippers' gardens were full of yachts' blankets being aired before going aboard for the season.

Besides the large number of Rowhedge men signing on in crews of yachts there were many others who had walked to Rowhedge from Tollesbury and West Mersea, seeking a berth in a yacht for the summer.

Saturdays or Sunday seemed most favoured days for the yacht owners to arrive to view their yachts in the various stages of fitting out. Many distinguished men have walked the street at Rowhedge including the Earl of Dunraven, Lord Gort, and King Olaf of Norway, but it wasn't always the yachts that took the eye of men of note; the fishing smacks to some were the most interesting. I remember during the First World War, my father was on the quay by his fishing smack *Beatrice* 156 CK, when he saw a naval officer coming towards him, together with a friend who was the late Sir James Dornville of Donyland Lodge. They stood talking to my father for a considerable time, asking questions about the smacks and fishing in general. I was told afterwards that the naval officer was no less than the captain of the battleship *Queen Elizabeth*. As the weeks passed more and more yachts were fitting out until the last of them had left Rowhedge, *en route* for the south and west coasts and some to the Clyde or even the Mediterranean. Very few, if any, of the wives would do their washing on the day when their husbands set sail down

Lord Gort's yacht *Thanet*, built by Harris Brothers, returns to Rowhedge to lay up for the winter. Captain Zach Burch and his crew are forward. Dr. Travers Kevern's last yacht, the smart little *Blonde*, lies at her stage in the foreground.

the river, because of a superstition. They thought it would be unlucky if they washed on that day as the saying was; "you would wash them away." We all knew what that meant when interpreted.

And now it would soon be May Lady Day. Many children including myself took part in going round with the May Lady. A few days before the 1st of May we would choose the hoop, then obtain two large flexible sticks, to form a canopy when tied to the sides of the hoop. As there were not many flowers in the gardens at that time, we would go up to the heath and pick cherry blossom, wood anemones and bluebells, but never may blossom of the hawthorn tree. Then, with a few flowers from our gardens and some given to us by friends, we were able to make our hoops look very pretty. So, on the eve of May morning, we found ourselves busy putting the finishing touches to our hoop display, sprinkling water on the flowers and hoping the weather would be fine the following morning.

It was pre-arranged who our individual May Queen would be, and waking early in the morning, each wearing a pretty dress, we eventually set out to the various houses at which we intended to call. By the way, there were just three girls to a hoop; the May Queen in the centre, under the bower (that was if we could keep the bower in position) and one girl on each side, so on a bright morning we would set off, perhaps as early as 7 a.m. If any boys saw us coming of course they would stand and laugh, but on we would go through the street, until we came to the first house on which we were calling. Incidentally we were usually very proud of our May Queen as she was more often than not the best looking one of the three of us. After some giggles and some misgivings we would arrive at our first house and sing our little May Day chorus, which was as follows: —

"Here we come with the May Lady, my father's gone to sea.

My mother's gone to fetch him back, so please remember me".

After that of course, we would knock at the door, and often we would be greeted with the words, "My dears, how pretty you all look, and your hoop too." Oh yes, sometimes we would get a copper or two or a little threepenny piece. After that we would go on our way to other houses, singing the same chorus and finally we realized that time was going on, so we had to hurry home after sharing the money, and then it was back in school at 9 o'clock so that was the end of that year's May Lady, as we always supposed it ended at midday. I only remember one Crowning of the May Queen ceremony, which was held at a fête in the grounds of Donyland Lodge, the home of Colonel and Mrs Holyrod. Mrs Holyrod, I remember, was a very gracious lady, but I must have been very young at that time as all I can recall is seeing the platform gaily decked with flowers, with steps leading up to it, and the May Queen taking er seat under the bower of flowers and waiting to be crowned; by Mrs Holyrod I presume.

By now, at the village school, Mr Barker and his teachers were preparing us for Empire Day celebrations. For several weeks we had been tuning up on patriotic songs, till at last the 24th of May was drawing near. That meant we went into the boys' school yard to do our marching and to sing the appropriate songs for the occasion and learn to "salute the flag" so that when the day arrived we had had plenty of practice. Out in the school yard we would go, piano and chairs were already placed under the tree ready for the onlookers who cared to occupy them. Looking back, it seemed quite an occasion and we as school children enjoyed it. The songs we sang I suppose helped to put us in the right mood, and they included such pieces as "Britannia the Pride of the Ocean", "Rule Britannia" and then we would march past and salute the Union Jack fluttering from the flagstaff and after singing the National Anthem it was home and a half-day holiday.

As it was now nearly the end of May, we as children found other enjoyments. The weather was warm enough to play on the marsh, so we felt that summer had come; the weather certainly told us it was so. On to the marsh we would go to play ball and run about, for there was a little bank on the first marsh and the remains here and there of a little blackthorn hedge, and one old dead tree. Well as girls, these little blackthorn stumps were very interesting to us. After collecting several laurel leaves, we would kneel by the stumps taking one or two prickles off them and start to do our "machining" as we called it. We would then prick the veins of the laurel leaves with a prickle which would be inspected by one of the girls who decided which one was pricked best. You will by now think that our pleasures were simple and so they were, as indeed they had to be, but we were contented. After the machining we would go to Three Corner; another part of the marsh, a wedge of ground enclosed with grassy walls between the first marsh and the river wall. Well, we knew that there was some pug (clay) on the Three Corner which was quite pliable, so we used to set to and work out a piece, making it into little ovens and saucepans and kettles. Reading about it in this day and age may sound very crude, but eventually we made those mud ovens which we called "dutch ovens", saucepans and kettles, and then the girls would spread out and pretend to get the dinner ready. When that meal time arrived each one inspected the other's "meal"; stones for potatoes, grass cuttings for cabbage, and larger stones for meat.

By the marsh wall just inside the first bridge gate, we held little "shows" which consisted of a piece of glass with heads of pretty flowers pressed on to it before being neatly covered in brown paper, with a lap on the front which we would uplift. The charge to see this was so many pins to come in the gate. So very childish you might again say, but enjoyable to those who took part. The boys were busy carrying their jam jars to the marsh, to catch tiddlers from the little pools left behind by earlier high tides.

So the days passed. The boys by this time were playing their game of cricket on the Three Corner and the girls were out and about with their dolls. Some had beautiful dolls, but they never came out to play, for they were kept in glass cases which stood either on the centre table, or side table in the front room of their house. Such a doll one of my nieces had. I still remember its pretty face; dressed in white silk and bonnet, under its glass case, it looked so attractive. It had to be taken care of because it had been given by the owner of the yacht of which my brother Jim was skipper, to his little daughter Audrey. Perhaps some more of those lovely dolls in Rowhedge at that time were given by yacht owners too.

Whitsun for many children meant the anniversary celebration at the Mariners Chapel. For many weeks they would be learning their recitations and practising their special hymns and anthems, hoping for perfection on Whit Sunday afternoon and evening when the Anniversary services were held. For many years Mr Flory of Colchester took those services, with Mr Harold Scrutton at the organ. How gratifying it was to them to see the chapel absolutely packed with people and I have seen people sitting on chairs and on the wall outside. The children in the choir dressed in new clothes and wearing buttonholes would be there taking their part; some a little nervous, others quite confident. A collection was taken which went towards the Sunday School treat. I mentioned the children's new clothes; it would not be an overstatement if I said the majority of the congregation wore new clothes too, and flower button holes. For several weeks prior to Whitsun, the dressmakers in Rowhedge were very busy indeed, one such person was Mrs Purle, who tried with her workers to please everyone by making their dresses ready for Whit Sunday, although some were disappointed. Dresses of course were more elaborate in those days with all the tucks, frills, and flounces, not like today's straight lines. Some of the children's dresses were made by Mrs A. Cranfield, and she usually did a little fancy work on them too.

My first recollection of being in the Mariners Chapel was of sitting on a form in class in the schoolroom with other very young children. I must have been very young indeed, but I remember how I was dressed. I had on a cream cashmere pleece* and cap and a little poke bonnet with two tiny ostrich feather tips in it. I evidently thought it was lovely as I have never forgotten it and I could only have been about two-and-a-half years old at the time, which sounds incredible.

With Whitsun over, it would soon be mid-summer, which meant that we could go on the river wall to tea. Many children, when they came out of school and if the day was sunny and warm, would go along the wall to play, and later many mothers would go along too, bringing their other children with them. In their basket would be sandwiches, sometimes shrimps, perhaps a little jam tart on a plate and a few buns. The mothers, who were usually in twos, then

*Cape.

proceeded to lay the table on the Three Corner; a nice even piece of grass was found and the table cloth was laid on it and the eats were spread around and then we would all sit on the grass to eat our tea. Tea, the beverage, was usually brought in jugs, and those who didn't like tea drank water. I, not having a mother, for she had died when I was nine years old, usually joined in one family circle or another and took my own tea. Everyone was kind in those days and those mothers were wonderful. "Aunts", who were not really our aunts, came and sat along the wall too, and when tea was over, or before tea, according to the state of the tide, children would go paddling, sitting with their feet dangling at the water's edge. Sometimes it even flowed on to the Saltings and it was lovely running up and down, splashing as we went. Boys of the village or at least some of them, would be learning to swim by the first "bridge", others along the "down street" wall and in the Roman River (Mill Creek). After we had eaten our tea and enjoyed our paddling, we would pack up and go home, and so to bed. Saturday mornings, when the tide was right, you would find many children "babbing",* either from the quays or from smacks' decks, that is if one's family owned a smack. Occasionally I went "babbing" from our smack but I don't remember catching many crabs. The ferry hard was always an attraction; children would paddle there on high tide, much to the dismay of the ferry boat man. When it was an exceptionally low tide, some would walk across the river to the Wivenhoe side. I did just that myself once, but only once. Sometimes, but not very often, there would be a little impromptu concert on a Saturday morning, in someone's garden shed or back garden. I remember going to one in a shed up The Road, which is now

The Scarlet Poms brass band and concert party at Rowhedge before 1914.

*Catching eels or crabs by placing bait on a line without a hook.

called Rectory Road. It was given by some older girls; they sang a few songs and tried to act a little but it was soon all over. Talking of concerts reminds me of the "German Band" as they were called, who came to Rowhedge some summers. The players parked their caravan on the marsh where the British Legion Hall now stands. They hired the room upstairs in *The Ship* which was a large room over the then billiards room. Performances were given in the afternoons after school. We paid to go in but I don't remember how much. The so-called artists sang and danced, and did a little sketch or two and then they would get the children singing and I remember one of the songs we sang was "Down by the river dwells Rosie Lee".

Something else which came to Rowhedge in those days were the Russian bears. They were really frightening to us as children. On long heavy chains they performed in the streets and the keeper would chant to them in muffled tones and the bears danced in their way and did tricks on a pole, while the keeper was hoping to get money from passers by. Rumours once went around that a bear and keeper had gone up into the wood at night, where he was intending to let it loose. Needless to say we all went home early but of course there was no truth in it, or at least the bear wasn't set free, as rumour said.

One summer, when I was about twelve years old, I had the opportunity during my school holidays to take a short sea voyage on board a cargo steamship whose captain was one of my cousins. I joined the ship at London docks and she sailed across the North Sea to Ghent in Belgium, to load cargo. I was fascinated by it all; the huge ship, so large after the smacks and yachts at home and the throbbing of the engines. I had a cabin all to myself near the bridge and ate at the captain's table. Holland and Belgium seemed strange countries to a small English girl. The people had strange clothes and hats, many wore clogs and smoked cigars, even small boys. In the streets were dogs harnessed to pull small carts, usually owned by milkmen and when the ship sailed through a lock, scores of children appeared and sang, hoping the crew would throw coins to them. I think some did. When she was loaded it was homeward bound back across the North Sea to the Thames. Of course, when I returned to Rowhedge I was the envy of many school friends and had to tell my adventures to them as though I had been on a voyage of exploration, as in our little world I had.

Well, the summer was getting on and it was Sunday School treat time. The church Sunday School in those days held their treats either on The Lawn or The Nursery of Donyland Hall. When the afternoon arrived we, the children, with our teachers, assembled in the school yard complete with new plimsolls and a mug or cup tied with tape around our necks. The Wesley Guild Band headed the procession up to the Church. Then came boys carrying banners; "God is Love" was one and "Feed my lambs" was another. We children in class followed up behind and into the church we went, where a short service was held. Eventually we again got in formation and headed by the band and banners we set out towards Jubilee (which is now called Parkfield Street) down Albion Street, along High Street, up The Road, now called Rectory Road, round by *The Ipswich Arms* and on to the Nursery, or along the avenue on to The Lawn, the band playing lively tunes to help us stick it out, I suppose. The first thing we did when we got to our rendezvous was to sit down and have a little rest as we needed it after that march. Afterwards we enjoyed the swings and played around until the races started. I am afraid I was never a sporty type and there always seemed a lot of pushing in the races — so much for sport.

Eventually tea time arrived, we sat on the grass and sampled all the eats that were offered. By now our mugs or cups were being filled with tea. At one such treat I remember the rector walking round stopping to talk to different children, enquiring how they were enjoying their tea. One boy wasn't at all pleased with his mug of tea and he told rector what he thought and threw the contents of his mug on the grass in front of him. The teachers and the bandsmen had their tea on the front lawn of the Hall and when that was over, fun and games restarted. The kiss in the ring game was very popular, also oranges and lemons. Eventually it was time to light the lanterns and trek homeward. The band again in formation, we would all march back to the school in wider lines, this time boys and girls arm in arm, eager to get back to the school to receive their bags of nuts and sweets. So the day ended, leaving hopes for another year. Looking back, I do think that the earlier form of Sunday School treats were enjoyed far, far more than the treats of today.

The Mariners Chapel treats were of the same pattern as the church, being held on the same meadows, but I do remember both church and chapel held one at least, perhaps more, on a meadow up Town Fields, now named Rowhedge Road. It was the same Wesley Guild band of Wivenhoe that headed the procession, followed by teachers and children of the Sunday School. The same games and races were played with tea on the grass. Somehow or other it was thought that the chapel did their treat a little better than anyone else's. The bags of nuts too were considered bigger by the children's standards! The fun and games would continue until the sun began to sink and the lanterns were lit. With the bandsmen in formation the march to the chapel would commence with the band playing lively tunes, all the boys and girls arm in arm and some carrying lanterns. We all joined in and it was hot and dusty but we enjoyed it so very much. As the procession neared the chapel, those who had lanterns (and incidentally those lanterns were so pretty) would get ahead of the procession and stand on the chapel walls, leading to the main entrance, to make an archway which the scholars walked under to go into the chapel to receive their bag of nuts and sweets at the end of the day.

SALTWATER VILLAGE

Autumn mornings brought mists lying close over the marshes and the river, usually lifting to fine days of which we made best use before winter set in. During September and October scores of yachts came back to lay up at Rowhedge, where most of their captains and crews lived. Others returned to Wivenhoe and Brightlingsea in the same way. Over the years at Rowhedge there were big racers like the *Yarana, Valkyrie I, Genesta, Rendezvous* and *Octavia* and fine cruising yachts like the *Merrythought, Island Home, Fiona, Reseda* and many others of all types, not forgetting the steam yachts like the *Pathfinder, Kempion, Walrus, Vanadis* and *Sunflower*, some of which were so big they had to lie in the mouth of Mill Creek, below the village, where the long sterns almost blocked the channel for the sailing barges.

The 386 ton steam yacht *Sunflower* whose captain and crew came from Rowhedge, steams away for her summer's yachting. Captain Powell and the owner are on the bridge and hands are working about the deck.

When all hands had got the yacht's sails and gear ashore and the cabins had been cleared of mattresses, bedding, crockery and carpets, etc., the yacht was often laid up on the mud above or below the village, with her bows in to the river wall, securely moored for the winter. Rows of all types of yachts lay there each year, waiting for the spring and fitting out. The crews were paid off but the captains and sometimes the mate had a retainer payment through the winter. For some of the captains of racing yachts this might be quite generous.

Sometimes a racing yacht came up the river flying her prize flags, won during the season's racing all round the coasts of Britain and sometimes also on the continent or in the Baltic as well. These were miniatures of the yacht's distinctive racing flag and were usually hoisted from the bowsprit up to the

A cruising yacht arrives in the Colne to lay up at Rowhedge for the winter. The skylights, deck seats, hatches and basket chairs were typical and the size and weight of her gear remind us of the work in manning and maintaining such craft. The owner sits aft with a camera.

masthead and often carried on down almost to the stern, if it was a successful boat. The captains and crews of racing yachts had a share in the prize money which the yacht won during the season and this could amount to a considerable sum. It was paid out when the yacht laid up, in varying amounts for skipper, mates, stewards and hands. As some of the big racing yachts had a crew of thirty or more, there were plenty to share the prize money but of course the amounts won were large by the standards of that time, £100 or £75 being a usual prize, with many cups in important races. The money was paid to the owner, who also had the cup or trophy, but the custom was for a large part of the prize money to be paid out to the crew as a sort of tip for their keenness and hard work during the racing season. This custom did not apply to cruising yachts, though sometimes the owners might give their captain and crew a present of money at the end of an enjoyable season, to supplement the wages. Many children received a little present when their father or brothers came home from yachting: a toy or a doll perhaps. Some men brought home portraits of the yacht painted in Italy and often showing Naples in the background, so I suppose most of them were painted there. Most houses in Rowhedge had these pictures, besides photographs of yachts and the crews, hanging on their walls until recent years. Sometimes there were also wooden half models, particularly of racing yachts, which were usually in the homes of their captains. They were made in the yard of the yacht's builder or perhaps by a relative who was a shipwright.

A typical painting of the yacht *Merrythought*, off Naples. Her captain was Jesse Cranfield. Most houses in Rowhedge contained at least one pair of similar paintings, brought home by village sailors from their voyages. Invariably one was in fine weather, usually with the Bay of Naples in the background.

My father was captain of several yachts, including the cutter *Nara* and the smart yawl *Reseda*, owned by Mr Leach, a shipowner in London whose ships traded to the Baltic and brought cargoes to Mark Brown's Wharf, near Tower Bridge. The *Reseda* cruised to the continent and the Baltic, and to other parts of England and Scotland. She was about fifty-five feet long and had a crew of four. Although they came from very different stations in life, Mr Leach and my father became friends in the way which many yacht skippers did. The relationship was not informal, nor could it be in those days, but it grew from a mutual regard; the owner for his skipper's seamanship and thought for his pleasure and interests, and the skipper and his crew for the owner's consideration and attitude as an employer, and respect for his obvious success in business. In this case it worked for mutual benefit as my father was able to recommend to Leach and Company many young seamen from Rowhedge for posts in the crews of their ships. This was a valuable connection for many, and some who had Mates and Masters Certificates benefitted considerably, eventually being in command of Leach and Company steamships.

With the smacks fitting out it was time for the annual village regattas; an important event in the Rowhedge calendar which I have written of in Chapter Five. Although there was little time for pleasure, the sailors' homecoming in autumn did have a little holiday air about it and at that time a smack owner might take his family down the river for a rare day's outing; women and girls

Rowhedge smacks returning up the Colne after a day's outing downriver with owners' families on board. In background the transom sterned *Unity*, owned by Mr James.

sometimes went on board their family's smack against the quays, but otherwise very rarely went afloat, except in a rowboat.

The dress and fasions of that time were not very suited to sailing and being afloat, and if a breeze got up and the spray began to fly things would get spoiled. There was then no ladies sailing wear such as the neat oilskins, shoes etc. available now, and of course these outings were only very occasional affairs. Anyway, sometimes we had a day downriver, going down on the morning ebb and after a quiet sail under suitable canvas, the smack might anchor under Mersea Stone, at the eastern end of Mersea Island, in the River Colne. While some went ashore for a ramble others might fish with hooks and lines brought for the purpose and the day passed in quiet pleasure until it was time to sail home in the evening. Sometimes a number of families would go down river on the same day and, returning on the flood in the almost calm of a September evening, each family would sing, the voices carrying across the water as the big harvest moon peeped up in the south east. People seemed to sing much more and more naturally then, perhaps they were more contented? On one such rare outing, when we were anchored off Mersea Stone in our smack *Beatrice* the anchor became foul of a large chain. While time passed, my father and brother Jack worked extremely hard to free it, for the tide was almost done. After desperate work at the windlass and with ropes, they freed it, but we always thought that Jack suffered permanent injury recovering that anchor because very soon afterwards he became ill and eventually died. He was a fearless sailor and racing yachtsman. His death plunged our family into deep sorrow.

Whatever had been earned during the summer yachting season had to be used carefully to help keep families during the winter, when money was scarce, as most of the village's seafarers were fishing in the smacks, stowboating for sprats. In the bitter winds and seas they toiled hard, usually for very small return and sometimes none. Occasionally lives were lost or smacks were wrecked.

A few Rowhedge men spent the winter going to sea in the crews of steamships. They chose ships which enabled them to return in the spring to sign on in a yacht's crew. Some larger yachts were away cruising and racing abroad, perhaps in the Mediterranean or elsewhere and their captains and crews were absent for the winter months, returning to refit in spring for the British season. A few young men from Rowhedge were sent to sea in big sailing ships as apprentices and some passed their exams to become mates and later masters. Many men studied navigation at the evening classes held in winter at the Nottage Institute at Wivenhoe. Some of my brothers studied there and these classes greatly helped local seafarers, shipbuilders and in later years amateur yachtsmen, and continue to do so, through the original generosity of Mr Nottage, a yacht owner who was its founder.

Many Rowhedge men sailed in the yawl *Glory* under Captain Chamberlain of Brightlingsea.
Here she sets her spinnaker while racing.

Many others were in the crew of the *Shamrock II*, one of Sir Thomas Lipton's America's Cup challengers. Captains Edward Sycamore and Robert Wringe from Brightlingsea commanded this 130 footer.

As the yachts laid up, more and more smacks were got ready, some out of the mud berths along the wall, where they had laid all summer while their owners and crews were away yachting. They were put on the ferry hard to have the bottoms scrubbed and to be painted and tarred. New ropes were fitted and the sails and equipment put on board to fit out for the winter's spratting, or stowboating as it was called because of the type of large net they used, known as a "stow" or "stowboat" net. The dark, small mesh of the stowboat nets was much closer than the trawls which were also used in autumn and spring.

The big stowboating anchors were being got ready and sometimes the long chain and rope cables for the stowboat gear were laid out up and down the High Street being checked over and prepared for the hoped for big catches. The spratting smacks anchored where the skipper thought the shoals of sprats would be and fished with the large stow net partly under the boat. Perhaps their knowledge, skill and luck would result in a good catch, which might be 300 bushels of sprats. Catching them was one thing but selling them for a good price was another. Many good catches meant that the price dropped and if the merchants and sprat curers at Brightlingsea, where most were landed, were full up with sprats, the fishermen could get nothing for them. Then the Rowhedge smacks usually sailed up the Colne to unload them on the quays to be sold for field manure and be carted away by the ton in carts to the farms. They fetched a few pence a bushel after all that hard work. There's no doubt that spratting in those days was usually heartbreaking work. Now one sees sprats in the shops sometimes at prices for a pound which would have bought many bushels in those times.

Some men dried (smoked) sprats in little wooden or brick smokehouses in their gardens. Hundreds of the selected fish were threaded on to tiny hooks which were hung on iron bars in the roof of the smokehouse, which was about seven feet tall and perhaps four feet square and often built of wood. A slow fire of oak chips and shavings was lit on the floor and the smoke went up around the fish. The secret was in controlling the fire and the amount of smoke.

My father was well known for his dried sprats, always of the highest quality, and Mr Leach found him a market for them at Gows of Broad Street, London. My father sent them there for many years, in neat boxes about three feet long by a foot wide, neatly packed, head to tail in fine tissue paper, all ready for display when the box was opened. When ready, the boxes had to be taken to Wivenhoe railway station to go on the 6.12 p.m. evening train for London, to be ready for sale the next day. Such were the quality of the sprats that my father had many imitators but no one could beat him at it. Of course sprats dried in this way fetched a considerably higher price compared to the tons of them unloaded on the quays when the curers at Brightlingsea could take no more.

In autumn and winter some of the smaller smacks worked at dredging

Small smacks dredging oysters on the Colne Fishery grounds at the mouth of the river Colne. A few Rowhedge smacks worked at this in winter but most were larger and fished much further afield.

oysters, usually in the river Colne on the Colne Oyster fishery, if the owners were Freemen of the River. Occasionally some of the larger smacks went fishing for scallops in the North Sea or down the Channel and some children got scallop shells and made them into little scales, with pebbles as weights and pieces of wood for the balance. One winter a big smack salvaged cargo from a wreck off the coast and it included children's musical instruments; so there were plenty of drum and bugle bands in Rowhedge for a time.

November brought the hazard of fogs, firework day and the onset of winter. Childhood's winter memories were the usual ones of snow and carol services, warm firesides and the bitter east wind. But the sigh of wind round the chimney and the bluster of a gale meant more to us than to children in other ways of life, for most of our fathers and brothers were at sea and we knew at such times they were facing its fury, perhaps hauling the nets in the smacks, standing watch on the deck of some great steamship in distant seas or working aloft in one of the big sailing ships. Perhaps unconsciously, always the sea was in the background of life, moulding thoughts and attitudes and eventually lives as well.

January had a special significance for me as my birthday was on its last day. Once, when I was about eight years old, a few of my little friends and I were enjoying my "party" in our house. Outside the wind howled and rain lashed down in torrents. Our smack, the *Beatrice*, was at sea with many others. We had just sat down to my birthday tea when there was a knock on the back door, which was opened to reveal a neighbour in gleaming oilskins and sea boots who had just landed from a smack with the news that the *Beatrice* had gone ashore on the Buxey sand, deep loaded with sprats. The consternation which followed completely ruined my birthday, but fortunately the staunch old *Beatrice* was got off by her crew and sailed home next tide.

If the winter was severe, as many of them seemed to be after Christmas,

Ice in the river Colne. ▷

children played the same games in the snow as they do today, making snowballs and snow men, while a few had improvised sledges. Sometimes the river froze. I don't remember it being solid, but large ice floes would accumulate after days of hard frosts and would sweep up and down in a grinding mass at every tide. This was greatly feared by the owners of smacks and other wooden craft lying at Rowhedge, as such ice can cause terrible damage to hulls. At these times most smacks would not come up to Rowhedge but anchored "in Colne", as the anchorage in the lower part of the river is known.

Some winters the moat at Donyland Hall froze and was used by local skaters, with the permission of the occupiers. Sometimes a big winter tide would flood Wivenhoe marsh opposite Rowhedge, and many skaters, accomplished and otherwise, would hurry there from Wivenhoe and Rowhedge to enjoy the fun.

At one time, early in this century, a village football club was formed called the "Rowhedge Star". Its committee sent out challenges to various teams in the neighbourhood and matches were played throughout the winter.

Winter evenings were occasionally enlivened by concerts and entertainments. Rowhedge had a concert party before 1914. It was successful for quite a time and people of the village enjoyed the concerts very much. The members were all natives of Rowhedge except two young men. The late Charles Simons was the comedian, always bright and cheerful in his everyday life too, only to be killed in France during the Great War.

There were sometimes what were called Smoking Concerts, which were all male affairs, usually organised by yacht captains and which many men of the village attended. The singing at these concerts was probably very good as in those days many men, particularly sailors, were good singers and took pride in

their ability, as sing-songs on board ship were a well supported entertainment. Their favourite songs were of course, of the sea and varied from "Spanish Ladies" to "Shipmates, Where Are You Sailing?" with its feeling of the roar of wind and tumble of waves. My father liked to sing and his favourites were "Jim the carrier's lad", a country song, "Under the British Flag" a patriotic one and, best of all, "Heave away on the trawl, which everyone evidently sang with gusto at these affairs. The words and tune were never written down but were handed on through the generations. My son John got a friend of his to write the music from a recording of the song made by Captain Harold Cranfield, and here it is:

1 "Oh once I was a schoolboy and lived at home at ease,
  But now I am a fishing lad who ploughs the raging seas.
  I thought I'd like seafaring life but very soon I found,
  It was not all plain sailing when we reached the fishing ground.
  It was . . .

  Chorus:
  Heave away on the trawl warp boys and let's heave up our trawl,
  For when we get our fish on deck we'll have another haul.
  So heave away on the trawl warp boys and merrily heave away.
  For it's just as light when the moon shines bright as it is at the break
    of day.

2 Oh, every night in winter, as reg'lar as the clock,
  On goes sou'wester, deep sea boots and oilskin smock.
  Then straight way to the capstan boys and merrily heave away,
  For its just as light in the middle of the night as 'tis at the break of day.
  It was . . .

3 Oh, when the eight weeks are over, hard up the tiller goes,
  Sou'west by west for Yarmouth Roads with the big jib on her nose,
  And when we reach the pierhead, the lassies they will say.
  Here comes our jolly fishing lads that's been so long away."

Some winter evenings we visited my grandmother Cranfield, who lived in a house "up the Cutt" (now West Street) which led off Head Street. This remarkable old lady loved telling ghost stories, if only to scare us on our way home; for she liked to make us sit up!

There is at least one haunted house in Rowhedge and this has been known by some for many years. Of course one cannot divulge its situation as the present occupants might not be aware of it. Relatives of mine lived in this house for many years and were never afraid of what they heard. Of course the boys of the family would from time to time say they had seen a ghost (a lady in white), in the back bedroom. Whether they were joking or whether it was a fact I don't pretend to know, but this story I do know — at least it was the experience of another relative of mine — when she called there one evening and was sitting talking in one of the rooms. "Oh dear!" she exclaimed. "Whatever was that?" "Well, now you've heart it you know it's true", said the young woman who lived there. It seemed like a mighty gust of wind coming down the stairs, that's all, but it had often occurred without any apparent reason.

Strangely enough, another ghost story circulated around the village when a family moved away some years ago. The building in which they had lived for years was suddenly reputed to be haunted. The man of the house said he had seen nothing unnatural while living there, but a tale was told which I cannot believe as it was never mentioned by grandmother Cranfield. An inn in Rowhedge, whose licence has long since lapsed, was used as a billet for troops during the English civil war in the 1660s. One New Year's Night two cavaliers quarrelled and in an upstairs room duelled to the death amongst the clash of swords and crash of furniture and pottery. Reputedly, each New Year's Night the sound of swords and cries are heard in the room as the unseen swordsmen repeat their duel.

So, on this eerie note we leave the village in winter, perhaps with the snow crisp on its streets and roofs and the smacks riding high on the tide, by the quays piled with heaps of silver sprats.

Sailing barges in the snow at the Hythe, Colchester's port at the navigable head of the river Colne.

The ploughman guides his team, a pair of magnificent greys, cutting brown furrows on the sloping fields of a village farm. This is probably Mr Cliff King from Fingringhoe, horseman at Battleswick Farm for many years, who ploughed there with horses until 1959.

CHAPTER FOUR

The Heath and the Wood

PERHAPS we could leave the streets for the time being, to walk through the heath and wood and take the same pathways as were there in yesteryear. So we will go up the road which leads to the heath and enter it by the little path, narrow even today, but the trees are much larger, of course. Oaks, ash and holly abound, and wild cherry blossom in bloom peeps through branches of other trees and as we go along we see glimpses of the "cuckoos" or wild anemones in flower and bluebells abounding too. Many children, myself included, have eaten the roots of the wild anemone. We called them "ground nuts", and liked to eat just a few. They did us no harm. Now we are out of the little path with all its curves and twists and on a small open space, so our next path will lead us to the pond and Green's Garden. No one ever paddled in the pond, or at least I never saw anyone doing so. It was the cause of some consternation in the village forty years ago as rumour got around that at mid-day the water in the pond turned to deep red. This soon died down so I suppose it was all a myth. And now to Green's Garden where once upon a time stood a large farm house. The driveway to it is clearly defined today, flanked by a Russian oak and Scots pine trees with a lilac here and there. On the west side are a few stumps of old fruit trees and a medlar tree that still blossoms. In this house lived the Green family who farmed the surrounding land until it was purchased by the War Department for Army use. I am not sure when that happened, but probably in the latter part of the nineteenth century.

We now pass through lots of undergrowth, hopping hither and thither, listening to various calls from other children, most of them out with their parents, for we would not feel at all lonely on these walks. The heath and the wood was like a Mecca to the people of Rowhedge, especially on Saturday evenings; Sunday afternoons and evenings too, after they came out of church and chapel. We almost knew whom we would meet in there, coming one way or the other. Well, we will imagine we are in the centre of the heath and have arrived at the wood gate, where two cottages stood. The huge field to the left was known to us as the strawberry field, for wild strawberries, very small but very sweet, grew there in abundance. Walking in the wood and to our left again, near the green path, was another old site where some family had lived in earlier years, for the fruit trees old and gnarled are still there, the only sign of earlier occupation. The green path was overhung with trees, and really beautiful mosses grew there and the new young green of the horse chestnut trees helped to enhance the surroundings. This was a young lovers' walk, indeed all the heath and wood was so and where else could be nicer, when the heart was young, with all the aspirations to which only youth and ambition can aspire. First loves and farewells find their way eventually into the lives of us all and I have no doubt it was so too in earlier years. So, hand in hand, let imagination take us to the bluebell carpet by the stream with its blue shimmer. How wonderful it all looked and how lovely to smell the aroma of the pines. We are now getting near to the west end of the wood and will soon arrive at the very small cottage which I was often told was made from the mud and clay from the Roman River, which ran only about 150 feet from its walls, whose construction is called "wattle and daub". The roof was thatched with the reeds that grew on the same river bank and I suppose what little timber was needed came out of the wood. I remember the elderly couple who lived there. The last time I saw them they stood framed in the doorway, smiling a little, nearing their journey's end, but standing there in their solitude, and letting the rest of the world go by. It is still a picture to me although I never knew this old couple, but I believe they were a Mr and Mrs Everitt.

We have now arrived at the further wood gate by the Mersea Road and must either right about turn and take other paths back through the wood and the heath, or come home to Rowhedge via Roman Hill and Weir Lane and skirt the woods. Roman Hill is part of the main road which runs 9 miles out from Colchester to West Mersea, another fishing and yachting village in days gone by, but which had few direct connections with Rowhedge.

There is a small green at the junction of Weir Lane with the Mersea Road and years ago an oak tree grew there which was reputed to have sprung from an oak stake driven through the buried body of a Rowhedge pirate who had been captured and hung in chains before being buried at this green; a grim story. The level field to the north of the entrance to Weir Lane became known as "the polo field" as the Colchester Garrison officers and their ponies often played polo on it before 1939. During the First World War I believe it was occasionally used as an airfield by the small aeroplanes of the time, flown by the Royal Flying Corps. Weir Lane runs through War Department (now Ministry of Defence) land. When a red flag is flown on the firing ranges at the Mersea Road end of Weir Lane or at the Wood Gate and near *The Ipswich Arms*, there is danger and no one should enter. Going towards Rowhedge, down Weir Lane, we come eventually to the small Three Corner Green opposite Daniell's garden. On this Green, I have vague recollections of festivities. As I was only six years old I can only remember seeing a little white pig in a small enclosure and people bowling in turn, so I presume they were Bowling for the Pig, and the celebrations were King Edward VII's Coronation Day, and the year was 1902.

Walking on, still skirting the heath on our right and Middlewick Ranges on our left, we come to a typical East Anglian cottage, with the roof at the back coming down almost to ground level. In earlier years it had played an important role in the life of East Donyland as it was then the village Post Office.

I wasn't aware of this until about fourteen years ago when it was told to me by my cousin, Captain Charles Watson, now a retired Senior Trinity House pilot at Southampton. He left Rowhedge with his parents as a boy to settle in Southampton and didn't pay a visit to Rowhedge for many years but when he did return he looked up all his living relatives, was welcomed by all and has paid us many a visit since. He told me that this Post Office at the heath was officially East Donyland Post Office and although I cannot remember who was postmaster when I was young, I recently discovered that during the 1880s a William Sargent was the "receiver" there and letters arrived at 3.40 a.m. by horse and cart from Colchester. After leaving this, its first port of call, it went on to take the mail to Fingringhoe, Peldon, and on to East and West Mersea. The journey was repeated in the early evening when mail was collected there at 8.30 p.m.

There was also a Post Office at Rowhedge itself, and again I discovered that during the 1880s a John Henry James was the "receiver" and letters arrived through Colchester at 8 a.m., with a second delivery at 2 p.m. which was sent via Wivenhoe. Letters were despatched from Rowhedge at 7.45 p.m. Any telegrams were sent from Wivenhoe Post Office. However, when I was young the mail came and went by train from Wivenhoe Station to Liverpool Street Station, London, the Rowhedge postman collecting it by going over the ferry to the station, night and morning. Harry Fairweather was the first postman that I can remember, and he held the job from a young man until his retirement. I recall how his ears got so frost bitten that they became thin and so poor Harry disliked the winters.

Today, the mail is again brought by Post Office van from Colchester. Oh, I have wandered from the path again, as we are really still on the heath, about to leave its Post Office, passing the main entrance to Middlewick ranges on our left and coming to the Cross Roads and *The Ipswich Arms,* "Barney's" as it is always called locally after one of its licensees, Barney Worsp. Another for a short time appears to have been Elijah Wade, who also owned the little smack *William Henry* which I mentioned lay in Saunders Dock along the High Street.

Well, perhaps you might guess that after the long walks and rambles through heath and wood and home via Weir Lane, or the other way round, many people would be thirsty and would stop and have a drink. Their wives perhaps would have one too outside and the children could have either a coconut or hard biscuit, whichever they chose. These biscuits were really first class, price ½d, and were practically the size of a standard tea plate. They

The *Ipswich Arms* public house, near the entrance to the Heath. Elijha Wade and his wife outside with their dog. A typical country public house.

were made by Mr Cheek, a Colchester baker. I known this in detail because when, later, my father became licensee of *The Royal Oak*, these biscuits were on sale there too. As you can imagine not all the people made a call at Barney's; most of them walked on down the road.

A few steps brought us to the main gates of Donyland House, today known as Heath House. The Daniell family sold it to Mr John S. Goodhart, a wealthy retired sheep farmer; perhaps from Australia or New Zealand. However, he lived there for many years before the First World War with his wife and son Eric. The war came and shortly after leaving Cambridge University his son volunteered to join the Royal Engineers. He became a despatch rider, had many narrow escapes and eventually came home on leave from France when after only a few days he became ill and died from a fever. His death was deeply lamented by his parents and he was given a Military Funeral in the old churchyard headed by the Band of the Royal Engineers from Chatham. The cortege left Donyland House, taking him on his last journey to the churchyard, his coffin draped with the Union Jack on top of which laid his cap. Many people from the parish, including myself, were there to pay their respects to a fine young English gentleman in his very early twenties, who was perhaps the most handsome young man I have ever seen in

A military funeral with coffin on horse drawn gun carriage, passing the thatched cottage next to the *Ipswich Arms*, on its way to the "old churchyard". Followed by mourners on foot.

my life, and I am certain there are many many more people in the village who would agree with this comment. Mr and Mrs Goodhart continued to live at Donyland House for some years and incidently Mr Goodhart was the first man to own a car in the village. I cannot tell you what make of car it was, but it was a very large one and open to wind and weather. One can picture them both in it, Mr Goodhart driving, his wife sitting beside him, always wearing a rather large motoring hat with a veil over the crown which came down over her ears to tie under her chin, as the car rushed along at 30 miles an hour.

Many of the later village Flower Shows were held in the field at the south east side of their house, and their own extensive gardens were always immaculately kept. Shortly after Mrs Goodhart died, her husband sold Donyland House and went to live elsewhere.

We will travel on a little further to reach Granny's Stairs, at the Rowhedge side of a bend in the road. These are concrete steps now, but in earlier days they were of earth, kept together by the roots of the oak tree that stood beside them. How the very name, Granny's Stairs, inspires one with thoughts of children's ways of life in earlier times. On Saturdays or school holidays we would walk up the road to the stairs, enjoying ourselves picking wild flowers from the hedgerow and peeping into the little nest of the robin which came to the same spot year after year, and finally playing on the nobbly old oak tree that was nearly dead. I wonder when and why this spot became known as Granny's Stairs, and who the Granny was. I am sure there is no one in Rowhedge today who knows.

The Road, which has now become Rectory Road, is today flanked by bungalows on one side and a Council estate on the other. We will pass Cricks Pond. There is no pond today, so no longer do we see children going over and over the iron bars of its railings. The Glebe Farm, which we are passing to our left, was demolished several years ago and today about forty or fifty bungalows stand in its fields.

Black bullace formed a hedge around the garden at the Glebe. They were planted there alternately along with white bullace. Many bought bullace at The Glebe when going to fetch milk from there; the black variety were 1d per pint and the white variety ½d per pint. These weren't considered to be at their best until the frost had touched them, which gave them a pinkish colouring. Besides eating them as fruit, or in pies and as jam, I expect some people made wine from them, as in those days many did from a variety of fruits; there was orange wine, elderberry wine, parsnip wine and many others, made from recipes and methods handed down for generations and it is interesting to see that home wine making has again become popular with many people.

Opposite the Glebe to our right is the Rectory, very little changed over the years. Walking on a few yards we come to a post-war, Council housing site to the right, with a few privately owned houses on our left. One of these is now named The Oaks. It was formerly a public house and my father became the licensee late in 1909 or early 1910. We didn't stay there very long and came back to one of the cottages in the High Street before war started in 1914. As a public house it was named *The Royal Oak*, and was quite a pleasant house. It had a small oak tree outside the front entrance, which led to the parlour. To this room on a Saturday evening came several men of the village, for a chat and a drink. It was quite comfortable with a large table in the centre, fitted across the top with black leather cloth and standing on it would be one glass and one blue jug, white lipped, more or less in line with each chair. It was here that a number of my uncles who were yacht captains would also come on a Saturday evening. They always smoked cigars and I thought the aroma lovely. The entrance to the tap room and bottle-and-jug departments was by side door; tap room to the left, bottle-and-jug to the right, and a billiard room upstairs immediately above the tap room. There were times when trade was very good and times when it could be very slack, especially in the daytime. I took no part in serving in the bars, for one thing I was too young to do so. At weekends the tap room did good business and many men came over from Fingringhoe including one farm worker, Old Thompson as he was called by everyone. He would sing the songs of the countryside and at the end of each

Looking down Head Street, with the *Royal Oak* public house on the left. My father was landlord from about 1909-1913. In earlier years it was kept by Jack Spitty, a noted fisherman and smuggler.

one did a clog dance. He would repeat this each time he came, to the amusement of the customers. We had in the tap room a Keith Prowse pianola and when 1d was put in the slot it would play a tune that you chose by dialling a certain number. Strangely enough, the only tune I can remember is "Boiled Beef and Carrots", which was rather brash but went down well with the customers and if Old Thompson was present he would be on his feet again in his hobnailed boots, dancing away in the same clothes he had probably worked in during his long day in the fields. After that, some would play darts or sing a song or two, drinking of course all the while.

In summer some men chose to play quoits on the stretch of land that adjoined the entrance and was owned by the brewers, Charrington Nichol and Company. The quoits pitch was about twelve yards long with a clay covered patch at one end about two feet square. In the middle of this patch was a stake which stuck up about six inches above the surface and over this the players tried to throw their quoit, which was an iron ring weighing perhaps six pounds.

Once a month it was pay-in night for those who were members of the Slate

Club, Mr Southgate was its secretary and as usual with such clubs it was share-out time shortly before Christmas.

In those days several public houses delivered previously ordered beer or porter in cans hung on a long piece of wood, four to five feet long, with nicks cut into its top at regular intervals for the can handles to be slotted into. Delivery time was just before 11 a.m. and again around 7 o'clock in the evening. Boys who were temporarily out of a job would do the rounds and there came a time when I took the job on too, so off I would set down West Street to call at the houses of the people who had ordered the drink. Most asked me indoors while they emptied the can and gave it back to me. Up the other side of West Street I would go delivering to other houses there and then, for me, it was back to *The Royal Oak*, to put the orders for Chapel Street on the stick. Then down the road I could be seen walking towards Chapel Street, first down one side and up the other. The delivery completed, I came back up the road with the empty cans, my job done except for washing up the cans, which had to be kept very clean and bright, and rubbed with silver sand to make them shine. Now I am certainly not inferring or suggesting that drink was supplied to practically every house. In fact many people were dead against all alcoholic drinks, and these cans of beer and porter were delivered only to people who had ordered them.

I was living at *The Oak* in 1911 when Halley's Comet was supposed to appear in the sky to the north west. Many of the inhabitants stayed up watching until late at night, our family included, but the comet never appeared.

John Spitty had been the licensee of *The Royal Oak* around the 1890s. He was a noted salvager, smuggler and fisherman, who fished from Rowhedge in his various smacks for a number of years. His smuggling led him to use many hiding places for his goods. Eventually he began to use one of the bedrooms to conceal boxes of smuggled Dutch cigars, building them up in furniture-like form which he then covered over with a chintz cloth and stood a mirror on top, with various dressing table accessories to complete the deception. The customs men suspected his cigar smuggling and searched *The Oak*. Mrs Spitty showed them into the rooms and cellars, and the so-called dressing table evidently escaped detection, but Mrs Spitty refused to let Jack hide any more smuggled goods in *The Oak*, so he must have found other hiding places, for smuggling in those days was not considered a social disgrace and very many local people were involved in one way or another.

I have been told many stories of Jack Spitty. When he wanted a quantity of coal he sailed his smack near an anchored collier brig or barge, off the coast, and shouted the apparently nonsensical question "Can you dress a hat?" The skipper of the collier, knowing what he meant, called to him to come alongside. Then the collier crew would open up the hatches and pass coal into

A typical photo of Jack Spitty, a Rowhedge smack owner and smuggler who was at one time also licensee of the *Royal Oak*.

Jack's hold, while his smack's crew gave them all the fish they wanted. The coal was used to fire the smack's shrimp boiler and for the cabin stove. I have heard it said that Jack Spitty's favourite saying was "If you were born to be drowned you wouldn't be hung"! He was a hardy seaman and once his smack was caught in a fierce North Sea gale, so strong that they set a storm jib at the mast instead of the mainsail. Jack battened the crew down below and took the helm himself. A big wave washed him overboard but the next one washed him back and when the alarmed crew came on deck they were off the Island of Heligoland.

There came a day when it was decided we would leave *The Royal Oak* and the licence was transferred to a Mr Cassell, early in 1913. A little way past *The Oak* a short cul-de-sac led off The Road to the north. This was known as The Cut but has since been renamed West Street. My Uncle Lemon Cranfield lived in one of the houses. He was apparently the greatest of all the great yacht racing captains having tremendous skill and success in making a yacht go fast and winning hundreds of races over the years. He had captained many yachts from the little racer *Cloud* to the large racing schooner *Miranda*, which was built at Wivenhoe, and the *Pantomime*; a strange name for a fast yacht, to the big cutters *Formosa* and the *Galatea* which was built to race for the America's Cup in 1886. The *Galatea* was built of steel and had a fault in her lead keel. Uncle Lemon and his smart crew of thirty could not make her go and after repeated trials he told the owner that she was not fit to race for the America's Cup, which is the world's greatest yacht race, so he resigned command and a captain from Dartmouth, who was not a racing man, sailed her across the Atlantic and raced her in America. She was well beaten, as had been predicted.

The moderate sized cutter *Neva* was his favourite command and with her he won the record amount of £1,335 prize money during one season; a fortune for that time. Of course in those days the captain was in sole command of the yacht and the owner merely enjoyed the sailing, not steering the boat. Sometimes he was not even on board during a race. Because of his success Uncle Lemon could afford to live well but his life changed and was saddened by the death of a son, drowned from a smack at sea. When I was small he spent his summers as the racing pilot in large yachts, advising the captain on the tides and currents, winds and lore of yacht racing waters all round the British coast, which he knew so well. In winter he fished and sailed his smack *Neva*, which was his pride and had been built from the prize money he had won in the racing cutter of that name.

We are now about to make our last three stops down The Road. On our right after passing West Street lies part of the Shipyard House garden and here also was the saw mill of the Shipyard. The previous sawyer was I believe a Mr Crickmore, but the earliest I remember was a Mr Foster and his son from Colchester. We could stand and look over the palings and watch them at work sawing away at large tree trunks, the older man on top (the "top sawyer"), the younger one underneath (the "bottom sawyer") in the saw pit, especially constructed for that kind of work. While this was in progress guinea fowl would be strutting in the gardens and when night came they flew into the trees to sleep. Chickens were kept here too, and it was the first time I had ever seen chickens with feathers on their legs. Later I learned that they were Buff Orpingtons, but they surprised me.

Now we look left down through an elm thicket and see the remains of the village's oldest cobbler's shop, lying really well back from the road in Chapel Street. It was built of red brick, had a pantile roof and in its dilapidated state one could peer through the roof here and there. I have looked at it several times and it seemed to me that the roof rafters had never been fashioned or planed down in any way but looked as if a tree had just been cut down and split lengthways in several pieces and then cut to size to form the rafters which I surmised were elm. Until recently, this old building still had the cobbler's name board on its front, but the name had worn off many a year ago. Mr Barrel was his name and it must been towards the end of the last century, or very early in this one, that shoe mending was carried on there. All these old landmarks are gradually fading away. Today this building stands no more. It was demolished, and replaced by a concrete garage with a room above it. Crossing to the other corner at the entrance of Chapel Street, we arrive and stay for a while at the first of the four cottages, because this was for many years where Miss Laura King kept her shop. Everyone in the village at some time or another was her customers, and again this was a front room which at all times was most tidily kept. As one walked in the door, cottons, buttons, tape, mending wool, and other things in neat boxes, would be on the right. In the centre of the room was a large round table where all the sweets were displayed, and facing you on the wall and also on the left side when entering, were many shelves lined with dark bottles and round boxes, some medium sized and some extremely small. This was HER chemistry department. Oh yes, it was so. In her own way she brought relief to people with the contents of the bottles that she made up for them for stomach pains and other aches. She also made her own ointments for skin troubles, and many people felt better after taking what she gave to them. Laura King, as she was referred to by everyone, was a very straightforward person and was always very correct when serving her customers.

At the other end of the row of cottages stood the shop and storehouse of Scrutton and Sons, who were noted as yacht painters and later also entered the building trade. For many years the shop's glass door panel proudly bore the engraving "Scrutton and Sons, yacht decorators".

Now we have come to the end of what we all knew as The Road which has since been officially named Rectory Road and joins the High Street opposite the Marsh Stile Gate, becoming Head Street.

CHAPTER FIVE

Flower Shows and Regattas

THE flower show was one of the major events of the year and given favourable weather was attended by almost all the inhabitants of the village who were at home. It was held in summer, at times on Donyland House meadow and in later years on the Brewery Meadow, towards the upper end, near the water tower. One can imagine the activity that went on during the evening before the Show. There were vegetables to be dug up and the choosing of this and that, which best to enter and the careful washing of exhibits before presenting them at the Show. Then there were the best fruits to be picked from the trees and polishing of jars of jams and marmalade and seeing they were still correctly labelled. There would be the jars of pickles too, awaiting their "beauty treatment". Then there were wild flowers and lovely grasses to be searched for, and keen eyes would be watching the gracious garden flowers hoping the weather wouldn't spoil them. Some of the exhibitors no doubt were anxiously wondering if their blooms would be just right when morning came; these of course weren't gathered until early morning of the Great Day. Then there would be the hopes and fears of the men who erected the marquees, hoping for a quiet night from the weather, which as we all know can play havoc with marquees. And so to bed, trusting for fine weather on the morrow.

The day arrives, and the exhibitors, in all haste, take their valuable cargoes to the Show tent, and are busily engaged in beautifying the space allotted to them for displaying their entries. At a specified time the large entrance flaps of the marquees will be tied back and after the Show's Official Opening, the public will make their way in, the aroma from the flower displays all-pervasive, so wonderful and refreshing. Put the clock back some sixty years or so and walk around the Show Tent. Memories will perhaps bring back to many the joy of those days. We walk into the tent, and immediately see the huge white wicker linen baskets in which the collections of vegetables were displayed. The superb quality of those vegetables was almost unbelievable and then there would be individual classes for all kinds of garden produce; potato class, cauliflower and cabbage sections, onions, celery, carrots, turnips, cucumbers, tomatoes, lettuce and many more varieties. Really the judges must have had quite a time of it deciding the award of prizes as the standard of the entries was near perfect.

I would share the laurels of the vegetable section between Stephen Cranfield and Harry Fairweather, both wonderful gardeners whose exhibits

The schooner yacht *Reindeer* was one of many yachts painted each spring by Scrutton and Sons, the yacht decorators. Here she beats to windward with Captain Cheek of Rowhedge at the helm.

were all grown on their own land. Each of them had most attractive flower gardens too. I think I'm right in saying that Stephen's pride was in his roses and cactus dahlias, when he lived at home with his parents at Vine Cottage. It had a large front garden, planted with rose trees. The back garden of the house was larger still, where he grew vegetables of all kinds and flowers too. I remember going up the back especially to see the dahlias in bloom, such beautiful specimens they were, and many mature fruit trees of all varieties grew there, including a fig tree bearing fruit.

I've wandered a little but am back at the flower show and on the very long centre tables were the various displays of flowers, beautiful blooms of many varieties, tastefully presented. Then we come to the basket of flowers section, so attractively arranged, looking so graceful, especially those in long-handled baskets. The wild flower section had a huge entry. There one could see wild forget-me-nots, honeysuckle, fox gloves, wild hyacinths, lords and ladies, and the fine grasses all intermingling, and in some of the jars even oak apples appeared.

There was also the class for individual rose blooms some of which were almost perfect, and the scent they gave off was lovely, as roses in those times were practically all sweet-smelling while most of today's roses, though lovely in colour and shape, are not very fragrant. We are now at the top of the table, so we will make our way down on the other side. Here would be the fruit section and oh, what wonderful collections these were. Soft fruits and plates of apples, pears and greengages and plums of many varieties, their natural bloom on them, and all this in the days when no spray was used. Next we would be at the home-made wines section and there were many first-rate home wine makers at that time. They seemed to make wine out of nearly everything, if it was suitable of course; blackberry, elderberry, mangel, orange, sloe, bullace. I don't remember who the prizewinners were but I do know there was keen competition. The cake and confectionery sections, too, found many competitors and quite a little rivalry, and it always looked so inviting and smelt lovely too. There were also countless sections for a variety of exhibits; fancy work in the form of petitpoint cushion covers, fire screen frontals, besides cushion covers in a variety of stitches. Many of them had a black satin background or plain linen, which appeared to be fashionable in those days. Crocheting too was a favourite pastime and when there was a collection of it on view at the flower show, it made one wonder how the women the patience to do such fine work in the intricate patterns. Some of it would be in the form of edging linen mats, afternoon table cloths and even along the tops of best bed sheets. The late Mrs G. Canham, in her earlier days Grace Barrel, was considered to do the best crocheting in the village; her work so even and spotless, too. Home-made and hand-made undergarments were among the exhibits. Oh, the gathers on the nightdresses, how carefully and consistently they had been stroked, and in some cases the garment would be finely tucked at the yoke if not embroidered, and embroidered again to form a frill at the wrist. Chemises had the same treatment as the nightdresses and were worn full length, and extremely neat hand work was put into these garments. I suppose I can comment on the third garment to complete these sets of undies, which was styled with a wide band at the waist and the length from waist to knee was gathered at the knee so that with the wide embroidery it gave them a deep frill effect. I might add that there was keen competition in this section at the Flower Show. Many women in Rowhedge would make by hand a whole set of these garments for just over 3/- a set or individually pro-rata. Considering the hours that were spent in making them and also that each garment had at least twice as much material as was necessary, it was cheap labour indeed.

The knitting section varied from men's socks to woollen garments of all kinds. I don't remember if there was a class for ladies' woollen shawls, for many women did wear shawls around their shoulders and some long ones too. The shoulder shawls were usually crocheted, I remember, but the larger kind were usually brought home from Scotland by many men who had been there in yachts which were manned from Rowhedge. Shawls! you might say. Today's cardigans and ponchos are surely only the modern version of them. I remember having a lovely soft wool Stuart tartan tam-o-shanter with a large pom pom on the top. I felt delighted when I knew it was for me, brought home from Scotland by my father, after a season's yachting.

We are in the flower marquee again viewing the school children's handiwork this time; darning on small pieces of flannel, men's socks, calico underclothes, pillow cases, specimens of button holes, sewn not floral and handwriting, all in competition but in individual classes. Mrs Barker was the school needlework teacher and how we had to stroke those gathers!

The canvas walls of the marquee was where the efforts of the men of the village were well displayed. Here would hang the cloth and woollen rugs that they had made during the winter months and really many of them were beautifully worked and the patterned materials used were from carefully washed discarded clothing. The woollen rugs that were exhibited were very cleverly designed and both they and the cloth rugs lasted for many a year. We see and hear of the rugs and fitted carpets that people have today even in their living room, forgetting that in earlier times cloth rug and canvas linoleum was the order of the day in most homes in this village, with woollen rugs in bedrooms.

Now, as far as my memory takes me, we come to the last section in the show which was floral table decoration. Each competitor was allotted a fair-sized dining table, entrants had to supply their own snow-white tablecloth and containers; some competitors chose opal glass. Looking along the line of tables, decorated to individual taste, one could only stand and admire. There would be one exhibit consisting of deep red and pale cream roses, displayed in a cut glass centre piece with four smaller matching vases, one for each corner of the table. Another exhibit would be the palest shades of pink and mauve sweet peas, in a container of silver log wood in effect, with smilax trailing from centre piece to each smaller container at each corner of the table. Another exhibit was of sweet peas and gypsophila tastefully entwined, yet another one of montbretia and pale marigolds, a heavier-toned display but very attractive in its way.

Now, I think I have shown you around the marquee to the best of my ability, so I hope you have enjoyed the tour, and we will step out into the open air, to listen to the strains of the Wesley Guild band on the meadow. This band came from Wivenhoe and presumably also played at all the treats in Rowhedge. However, I do remember one occasion when a fair came there, but whether it was for Flower Show Day or Regatta Day is not quite clear to me. It was Barker and Thurstons Fair of Norwich and it stood on the Brewery Meadow. All the fun of the fair was there in grand style, with roundabouts and gondolas, swinging boats, coconut shies, shooting galleries, confetti and squirts* (which no one liked), a tell-your-fortune booth, and the organs on the roundabouts playing popular tunes of the times; which all made for fun and frolic. How many days it stayed on the meadow I do not know, but I do remember that things nearly came to grief. It had rained heavily during the night and when the fair was due to leave in the morning, the meadow being of a soggy nature it truly lapped it up. When morning came, the fair was all packed up and ready to move but nearly all the heavier vehicles couldn't get started, so they tried to get them out with one of the fair's traction engines. This was repeated once or twice, and at the next effort the traction engine got bogged down and all the hands of the fair started to dig it out. But dig as they might, it was to no avail until at last with heavy ropes around it and with the men still digging and pulling, the engine started to move forward until it came out into the top of Albion Street. It was real herculean effort; but the fair came no more to the Brewery Meadow.

Back to the last frivolity of the Flower Shows, which meant dancing in the precincts of the water tower grounds, all lit by lanterns, with plenty of happy dancers having their final fling of the day, to the strains of the Wesley Guild band. Then it was home for everyone. Were those the days? I think they must have been.

However, the regatta was the principal event in the village year. To start to recall them, oh dear, what memories are conjured up in one's mind! I had better start by referring to the placards, for under the heading of ROWHEDGE AND WIVENHOE REGATTA came the words "Under the Patronage of King Edward VII" and later, after King Edward VII's death, King George V became the Patron. You see, Captain John Carter, then of Albion Street,

*Jets of water with small balls floating on top, which were shot at for prizes.

Rowhedge, was captain of the King's racing yacht *Britannia*. He served under both King Edward VII and King George V and one can only assume that was how the Royal Patronage came into being.

At that time the regattas were a combined Rowhedge and Wivenhoe event and were held at each village on alternate years. This continued up to 1913. In those days regattas were held much later in the year than they are now. There was of course a reason for this, as the local men were away yachting until September came in. I remember that the 1908 regatta was held during the first week of October. I remember it so well, but so sadly because my brother Jack lay seriously ill at that time and he had always sailed and raced in the regattas. Each alternate year, both at Rowhedge and Wivenhoe, there would be a fine display of fireworks which were lit at the end of the day, erected for Rowhedge on the opposite side of the river at the ferry crossing, and for Wivenhoe on the Fingringhoe bank. Money for the prizes, fireworks and the few other expenses of the regatta was collected by a committee. Looking up some records I find that, for instance, the 1904 "Rowhedge and Wivenhoe Regatta", as it was called, was held at Rowhedge on 15th September. The subscription list was headed by King Edward VII with £10, followed by the Prince of Wales (later King George V) with £5 and the remainder of the list was made up by the ship and yachtyard owners, tradesmen, shopkeepers, and a good number of seafarers of the village, including yacht captains and others, backed up by a few local gentlemen. That year £116. 15. 6d. was collected and after the regatta a balance of £25. 8. 8d. remained.

First we must dwell awhile on the activity that went on prior to The Day. As you can imagine practically every boat had to have a once-over from their crews, to see the ropes, etc., were trustworthy and as for the smacks entered for the Smacks Race, well, practically every one of them was put on the ferry hard or at Pearson's Quay to have their bottoms scrubbed. More than one was blackleaded, the idea being that it made a boat slip faster through the water. When all these things had been done and The Day was nearer, on the ferry hard men would be arguing out in theory who would be the winners of the various races. Not only were there the smack races, but also races for smaller yachts, sailing dinghies, rowing boats and gigs, the rowing club's galleys and rum tums,* and other types of sailing craft. All races attracted quite a lot of entries which was very gratifying to the committee.

We will now imagine that it is the eve of The Day and will stroll down to the ferry where strings of yachts' flags are flying in the breeze. As many smacks and sailing boats went down the Colne the night before after loading up with food and suitable racing gear, they would leave on the tide, hoping for a fine day and a good breeze on the morrow. For the rest of us it was to home and bed, or perhaps just up to the Marsh Stile Gate to see the finishing touches

*Fast rowing boats, sometimes used for racing.

being put to the fair. Oh yes, it came each year, quite a big affair it was too; Barker and Thurstons again. There would be the roundabouts, one with cocks and hens to ride on and gondolas on the switch back; the latter appeared in our minds a very risky thing to go on, but those ideas changed as time went on.

When Regatta morning came the first thing to be weighed up was the state of weather, including which way the wind was. We always weighed that up and hoped it was favourable to those racing — a fair wind home so the boats didn't have to tack on the homeward part of the race up the river.

After an early dinner we prepared to take our seat in a smack's row boat. Many went in boats in those times and these boats were tied up alongside smacks that were not racing. I rather liked it that way, but that's not done these days. Spectators walking along the street would find the Wesley Guild Band playing on the quayside, the pubs all open and sounding as if they are doing good business. Eventually all who intended to sit in a boat took their seats and their vantage point. After a couple of hours viewing that way one could always step ashore and stroll along the street with the crowds. I cannot remember which classes of boats were first home, so I presume it would be the rowing and sculling races, rowboats, galleys and rum tums that were the earlier ones on the list. Swimming races were highly competitive. My brother George (Tim) was evidently the champion swimmer. So much so that after a

Regatta day 1909. The bandstand on Pearson's Quay. The committee smack *First Fruits* lies on the Wivenhoe bank, with the set pieces for the fireworks beyond. The white shed on Wivenhoe marsh was where Mr Humphrey built his aeroplane.

time the committee asked him if he would stand down, and he did just that, for no matter what handicap they put on him he beat all comers. Before standing down he had won some valuable prizes in silver; a beautiful silver teapot, sugar basin, butter dish, and tray; so many that he made himself a display cabinet to keep them in. I saw them all recently, all in excellent condition and lovingly cared for by his family.

Now the smacks were getting nearer and the crowds on the quays and on the Wivenhoe bank soon sighted the first of them. Much guessing would be going on among the crowds as to which boat was lying first at that point; nearly home so far!! But, even today, a calm seems to come about when sailing up river past Harris's Shipyard (now Ian Brown Ltd.), which put paid to more than one hope of winning. I suppose it is safe to say that the smack *Neva*, owned and sailed by Lemon Cranfield, would give a good account of herself and many times she got the first gun when passing the ferry hard, proudly under a cloud of canvas. At the gun the cheers would go up and the band on the quay would strike up to put everyone in a good mood.

I remember one such smacks' race about 1904. I was with my mother down by the ferry to watch the smacks come home and enjoying it when, to our amazement, we saw my brother Jack (John O.) standing on the cross trees up the mast of a racing smack about to pass the finishing line. When we saw him standing there we were filled with anxiety in case he should slip, but he didn't.

Smacks racing in the regatta 1904. The *Elise* (Captain Green) and the *Maria* (J. Gunn) both from Wivenhoe, and Captain William W. Cranfield's *Sunbeam* from Rowhedge, furthest from camera.

After all the sailing events had been raced and one or two spills out of the unsteady rum tums, it was time for the "Pull Devil Pull Baker" event. Two boats, smacks' rowing boats, with their crews of five per boat would pull out from the ferry, then be tied together some seven yards apart each with their precious cargo—one had a large box of bags of flour and the other boat had soot. When in the middle of the river the race would start and quickly gain momentum. The soot and flour fell thick and fast, the crew who received the soot looked like black men, and the flour men looked like bakers. So the throwers notched up several hits. I don't know how it was decided which were the winners of the race.* After this race the water looked very grimy and incidentally the "Pull Devil Pull Baker" is still to this day an event in all local regattas.

Then there was all the fun of the fair to look forward to, with various degrees of excitement depending on one's age, and later the prizegiving, with cheers and clapping for the winners. At dusk came the fireworks, with rockets and set pieces fizzing by the riverside, always ending with a portrait of the King. Then the crowds broke up, the younger ones to go back to the fair and many older ones home, with much talk of the day's doings and of previous regattas; of who had won and how others lost. It was an enjoyable day for all.

The Rowhedge regatta was revived for two or three years immediately after the First World War, but then lapsed for many years until it was again revived in 1962 and has carried on since as perhaps the most popular regatta on the River Colne, with scores of sailing boats and even a race for some surviving smacks, which come mainly from West Mersea and Maldon, with one or two from Wivenhoe and Brightlingsea. Some of them still set a topsail and remind older ones of the stirring sights of the old village regattas.

*The "race" was won by the first boat to tow its opponent's boat, stem first, over a short predetermined distance.

CHAPTER SIX

Streets of Sailors

NOW we leave the High Street and the waterside and go on our way up Albion Street. Passing the *Albion Hotel* we also pass the four cottages that always had black water butts alongside their front doors. The back way to these cottages is or was known as Stone Alley. A little further up on the left lived my Uncle Turner Barnard and his wife with their family of three sons and seven daughters. He lived much longer than any of the Barnard brothers, dying at the age of ninety in 1932. Besides owning the smack *Prince of Orange*, he was captain of several cruising yachts. One of these, the 100 foot *Bridesmaid*, was involved in a race to the island of Madeira in the Atlantic, against a yacht named *Atlantis*, for a wager between their owners of £1,000. News of the race came as the *Bridesmaid* lay off Southampton. The mate went on board with a letter of instructions from the owner to get the yacht ready for an ocean race and enclosing the course details. This incident became well known and emphasised Uncle Turner's calm outlook and is one which sailing people will enjoy. "Start off Hythe, leaving Calshot light to starboard and going out of the Solent by the Needles channel," read the mate. "Proceed to Madeira and finish off the fort. Distance approximately 1,300 miles." "Hmmmm," said Uncle Turner, staring thoughtfully at the deck. "Do that say anything about luffin?".

A cholera epidemic threatened the district one winter when the *Bridesmaid* was laid up at Rowhedge and Uncle Turner had the yacht hurriedly re-rigged and sailed her down river to lie in the Colne off East Mersea for a few weeks with his family on board, the children enjoying this unexpected holiday from school. He was later captain of the large square-rigged steam yacht *Fedora*, owned by Baron Newborough, and sailed her out to cruise in the East Indies with a large crew, mainly from Rowhedge. They had some strange tales to tell of far away places when they returned; of monkeys and parakeets, head hunters and land crabs. Turner's son, Henry Barnard, sailed in the crew of the *Fedora* and later rose to be captain of merchant steamships.

Across the road lived Captain Zach Burch of the cutter yacht, *Thanet*, owned by Lord Gort. A few steps further on and we are at Genesta Cottage, the home of Captain John Carter. When captain of the *Genesta* he sailed her in America as challenger for the America's Cup in 1885, but without success. Later he was appointed by King Edward VII to be captain of the new royal racing yacht *Britannia*, and when he in later years retired from yachting, his

Finish of a smack race. The Wivenhoe smack *Elise* (Captain Green) and the Rowhedge *Ellen*, owned by Uncle Richard Cranfield, sail to the finish past Harris Brothers yard with only six feet between the ends of their bowsprits after racing a 22 mile course.

The royal cutter *Britannia* sailed by Captain John Carter and the *Ailsa*, sailed by Captain Tom Jay, both of Rowhedge, with crews mainly from the village, racing in the Solent.

eldest son, Captain John Carter, who then lived at West Cowes, took over from his father, also to become captain of *Britannia*. After several years, he was followed by Albert Turner of Wivenhoe who, until he was appointed skipper of the *Britannia* (in the days of King George V) had been captain of Sir William Burton's many fine racing yachts, and it was then that my brother James Barnard was engaged to become captain of Sir William Burton's yachts.

Over on the left side of the road there was living at home, with her aged parents, Miss Louise Gredley. A tall stately personage, fair of face, golden hair always most beautifully dressed in any style that was fashionable at the time. At all times she was correctly dressed and wore her clothes with dignity; charming! The lovely hats she wore, too. I am still able to vizualise her in her silk or voile summer dresses, with which she would sometimes wear a large black tagee straw hat with the loveliest of silk roses around the base of the crown, or perhaps it would be a hat of lace, or leghorn hats adorned with black (1 inch wide) velvet and cherries to the side. At other seasons of the year she was just as attractive in heavier clothes. Then Miss Gredley wasn't old, oh no, thirty at the most, I should say. She was a friend of my sister Hettie, had

The 98 tone yacht *Bridesmaid* which Uncle Turner Barnard skippered during her ocean race to the island of Madeira, against the yacht *Atlantis*.

many other friends, and was also one of my school teachers. However, there came a day when Miss Gredley married and went to live at Halifax. I suppose she did re-visit Rowhedge when her parents died, but after that she came no more.

Still in Albion Street and a few more steps up the hill we could perhaps have met another person, named Emma Boyston, who lived in a cottage with her mother. They took in washing and in their way worked very hard. Emma would run errands for people and would nearly always be talking to herself. As often happens to such people she received a great deal of unwelcome attention from quite a few boys of the village. What they used to call out after her seemed to me ridiculous; they would keep on shouting "The blooming pump is broke again. Emma, the flames are up!" I suppose that originated from the day when the pump at the top of Jubilee broke down and Emma couldn't draw water from it, which probably got her so mad that she shouted out "The blooming pump has broke again".

Albion Street figured in a nineteenth century smuggling story. Some smugglers had landed a cargo of smuggled goods in the village but the revenue men were after them and eventually they were at their wits end for a safe hiding place as the houses were being searched. One smuggler remembered that an old smuggler who had been very ill lay dying at his house in Albion Street. With the agreement of the family the cases of goods were secreted

Looking up Albion Street. The Coronation Bakery angled at the top and a baker's cart in the street.

under the old man's bed and he was told of the contents. The revenue men came up the street rummaging the houses but when they heard the old man was near death they merely peeped into his room, to see him propped on pillows, before going on up the street. The story goes that the old smuggler died shortly after the cases had been safely got away, with a smile on his face at having outwitted the revenue, even at the end!

The last house to notice in Albion Street is where Captain Isiah Powell of the *Sunbeam* lived with his wife and family. Mrs Powell was quite old but she would still be serving in her little general shop, which was in the front room of the house. On the floor could be seen stacks of old newspapers which grew higher and higher so that she could scarcely lift her feet high enough to walk over them to go to the counter to serve any customer. Why she ever bothered to keep a shop I can't fathom; there certainly was no financial need to do so as her husband was captain of Lord Brassey's yacht *Sunbeam*, which meant money, and he had seven houses built in Albion Street and four more in Regent Street. Well, be that as it may, Mrs Powell was quite a nice looking person for her age with her attractively curly hair. Of Captain Powell, personally I know nothing; he must have died around the turn of the last century. The last houses he had built in Regent Street are dated I.G.P. 1899. However, I do know that he was captain of the *Sunbeam* when she sailed around the world during 1876-1877 and that her crew of 29 included 14

Captain Isiah Powell of Rowhedge commanded Lord Brassey's steam auxiliary schooner *Sunbeam* during her voyage around the world, and most of his crew were from the village.

Rowhedge men. She did come to the Colne when I was young but I don't remember ever seeing her. From photographs and pictures I have seen, she was a fine, square-rigged yacht with three masts, a topsail schooner, and had a yellow funnel for her steam engine. She was certainly a very beautiful craft. Lord Brassey had her for many years and Lady Brassey wrote a book on her voyages.

We are now at the top of Albion Street where it forks. To the left is Jubilee, now known as Parkfield Street, and to the right is Paget Road. I think we had better travel Paget Road first as there is only one thing to write about; the Paget Memorial Cottages, erected in 1889. There is a white stone tablet at the lower end of the cottages which states:

"In Loving Memory of
Lord Alfred Henry Paget
Son of
1st Marquis of Anglesey, K.G.
This building is erected by Cecelia, his wife, June 1889"

There are four dwellings in all, which are still owned by the Paget family and were built to be occupied by yachtsmen and their wives; the men earlier in their lives having served either in the first Marquis of Anglesey's yacht *The*

Jubilee (now Parkfield Street) looking towards the "pump gate" before 1914. Many roads in the village were then unsurfaced with tarmac.

Paget Memorial cottages in Paget Road. Built by the Paget family for their aged yacht hands. Now renovated and still providing good homes.

Pearl, which was built at Colchester in 1818, or on his son, Lord Alfred Paget's many subsequent yachts. Today they are occupied and are granted to applicants who can qualify as being descendants of the older generations of yachtsmen of Rowhedge. Thoroughly modernised around ten years ago, they are now likened to first class flats; re-roofed, ceilings lowered, with bathroom, wash basin, hot and cold water and toilet in each dwelling, where the kitchens have been modernized, with an up-to-date fireplace in the living room and painted beautifully inside and out. Once the occupiers have been granted permission to live in them, there is only one restriction they must comply with, which is that each occupant must hang the supplied framed photograph of Lord Alfred Paget on one of the walls of the dwelling they occupy. The rent is free, the tenant only paying rates, which are nominal. So with a good Christmas hamper sent to each one of them annually, the occupants of Paget Memorial Cottages have every reason to be grateful to the skills of their forefathers, knowing they have a good roof over their heads for as long as they live.

We will now travel along Jubilee, or Parkfield Street as it is today, where there are quite a number of nice houses, the most outstanding being Tring House, the home of Mr and Mrs L. Southgate. Very pleasant in design, and always so neat and tidily kept, both house and garden, one cannot but admire it. Certainly I do, as part of it is built on the garden my father once owned and

101

where he had intended to have a house built around 1903, all hopes of that being dashed when my mother became seriously ill and passed away in 1905. There we grew all kinds of vegetables and gooseberry bushes, red and black currants. Fruit trees included black plum, greengage, apple and a fine William pear which practically every year would give a good yield. William pears are luscious aren't they? And up to this day this same pear tree brings forth its harvest, as I have a peep at it from time to time; sometimes it is sweet to remember. Leaving Tring House and its garden, we arrive, in theory, at the pump and Pump Gate, long since demolished, and so in imagination we will turn sharp left from the pump gate and after going through the first kissing gate, walk slowly over land now dug as sandpits and pass the dove house on our left. It was quite a huge one, built in the same kind of bricks as Donyland Hall. Called "the duffus" by locals, it was partly demolished about forty years ago and some of its foundations were incorporated within the foundations of a new bungalow.

We will go through the next kissing gate and take the path along The Lawn to the right. On our left would be a farm worker's cottage and a cluster of farm outbuildings of Donyland Hall. Yet another kissing gate to go through and then we reach the avenue leading to Donyland Hall. Walking up its right side we come to the main gate which opened into Fingringhoe Road. The gate, by the way, was always open. As we right about turn we find just off the path a

The kissing gate at the upper end of Church Hill, looking into the village towards the church.

small natural pond and a little further down the horse pond; memories of summer evening walks and winter ones too are now just memories for only the few of us who are left, with skating on the horse pond in winter when the ice was thick and winter reigned.

We are now at the Hall; I'm not sure when it was built, but probably a bit earlier than Elizabethan times, surrounded by gardens which slope down to the moat. In springtime the primroses and violets peeping out here and there on the grassy slopes looked so lovely. Several families have lived at the Hall within my memory. The Robinson family, the earliest I can recall, were always spoken of as the finest farmers in the district, to which they could lay a just claim. The next occupant was a Mr Miller, then came the Webb family, and later on Mr D. A. Green. It was he who bred those beautiful Suffolk Punch horses, in quite large numbers. When let out of the stables they would gallop down the chase on to the marsh, where the large sheds of the Wharfage Company now stand. What a sight it was to see three or four pairs of glossy flanked horses at work ploughing the fields around the village and hear the straining of harness and the encouraging calls of the horsemen. The plough-shares turned furrows as straight as a ruler and men and horses were followed by clouds of squabbling gulls and peewits fighting over worms and insects in the new-turned field.

In the late 20s or very early 30s, the sandworks bought the fields of Donyland Hall; all but The Lawn, one field along the Pightle and two others skirting the Fingringhoe Road were dug out for sand and ballast. The next occupant of the estate was Captain Lindsay Smith, who must have spent a fortune on restoring the Hall, its outbuildings and gardens, and building the cow sheds in the most up-to-date manner. No expense was spared, he being very wealthy, but he did not live long enough to enjoy the results of his dreams. When he passed on, the estate was sold, and the present owner is a Captain Thistlewaite.

On our way back we are coming along the lawn path, and on our left we pass the huge chestnut tree, still standing. In days gone by it always gave a good yield, so around October there would be chestnuts galore for anyone passing by. We will now turn to the right and go down the chase which led to the marshes.

The dove house was reputed, with good reason, to have been a hiding place for smuggled goods as late as the end of the nineteenth century. The late Mr Oscar Lay could recall that smacks' boats loaded with contraband were rowed up Mill Creek, as the Roman River is locally known below Fingringhoe Mill, and the goods were landed at the river bend at the foot of this chase, up which they were carried to the dove house by those in the know, to be distributed later. In earlier times smuggled things were also landed further up the creek and were reputedly carried inland in farm carts, as the farmers were

103

in on it too. Much of this went to Tiptree Heath, which was a distribution centre for Essex smuggling for many years. This illegal use of Mill Creek probably caused the spread of the local ghost story of the "old man who shakes his chains" along the footpath called the Pightle which runs from Fingringhoe Mill to the south end of Rowhedge High Street, at the black gate. No doubt the smugglers encourage this to scare off anyone from investigating too closely any flashes from dark lanterns, clinking of bottles or movement of men in that area when there was no moon but the tide served, which is when the smuggling runs were made.

Sailing barges often went up Mill Creek with grain for Fingringhoe Mill which was owned by Chopping Brothers. The old part of the mill was built of wood across the head of the creek, after which it was known as the Roman River. The machinery in this part was driven by a wooden water wheel. A more modern part of brick had been built on to this and had machinery driven by a large steam engine whose thumping could be heard a mile away, when it was running. A very tall chimney kept the sparks and smoke away from the mill, but this was demolished years ago.

The field to the left of the chase was often set with khol rabi plants. Walking down there one evening with my girl friend and two boys from the village, they went into the field and pulled a khol rabi for each of us. After they were peeled we all tasted them and found them a bit sweeter than a turnip, but after a couple of bites my friend and I formed a poor opinion of them.

Years ago, long before I can remember, the Bruce family lived at Donyland Hall, and I would like to tell this story. A Miss Bruce married a member of the Ismay family and they made their home at Doorpool, West Kirby, Cheshire. About the same time Alec Bruce, of The Hall, married a first cousin of mine, Clementine Cranfield. She was a very tall and stately person, six foot tall, and with the carriage and walk of a queen. I imagine that she was not what one could call pretty, but one wouldn't pass her by without remarking on her regal figure. They too went to live in West Kirby by the shores of the Dee, at Ring o' bells Road, near the mansion named Doorpool, where the Ismays lived. I don't know how many children there were in the Ismay family but one became Sir Bruce Ismay, Principal of the White Star and Cunard lines. Well, be that as it may, ill health overtook Mr Alec Bruce and when still a fairly young man he died and lies buried in the Ismay's family vault at Anfield Cemetery, Liverpool. After a short while Mrs Clementine Bruce returned to Rowhedge and lived there in a house in the High Street until the end of her days, her circumstances much reduced, for she had seen better times, but in her widowhood glad to come home to the village.

I have recalled the lovely walks we enjoyed on the Donyland estate and I am sure for many generations before I was born, villagers also walked its paths. None of its gates were locked, and Rowhedge people looked upon the right to indulge in these walks as theirs. However, there came a day in the 1920s when everyone learned that the right of way through the Donyland Hall estate was theirs no more. After how many years? I wonder!!

Back in the village again, along the High Street, near the ferry hard is Church Lane. Just a little way along it to the left there were two cottages. A very old lady lived in one of these named Mrs Taylor, always known as "Rattles". Children would often congregate outside her cottage, seemingly for no reason except to annoy her by calling out. Sometimes she would stand no more of it, and would open her bedroom window and pour out the contents of her night pot, hoping some of the culprits would get wet, and which splashed them from time to time, as I have seen it happen when standing quite a distance away on the other side. Often it was a good thing when the school bell rang. On the opposite side of the road there were four more cottages, the first of which was where Mrs Betsy Everitt kept a sweet shop. She was very strict, conducting the business of her little shop, standing no nonsense from any quarter. I know she made lovely "stick jaw" and homemade toffee, and sold strips of liquorice, ever-lasting strips, and hanky-panky at ¼d or ½d a portion. Many a day children hadn't even these tiny amounts to buy sweets, for we certainly didn't have a sweet every day, by no means. However, a good substitute for them was made by putting moist sugar flat on a thick piece of paper, and pressing a red hot poker quickly onto the sugar, taking care not to set the paper alight. Burnt sugar we called it, and it was very nice too.

Church Lane is noted for one thing; its high linen lines which help people to get their linen dry quickly. The linen lines are attached to and are worked by pulleys, the height provided for them by poles made from yachts' old topmasts and other spars, and this goes for other parts of the village too. All the poles were well stayed and the rigging on some was elaborate. On Sundays and public holidays it was the custom to fly a flag from many of the linen poles; usually a yacht's ensign, sometimes a Union Jack and some seafaring householders, if they were at home, would hoist a burgee to the "masthead" of the linen pole. Unfortunately this cheerful custom has now almost died out.

Church Lane had its smuggler's houses too. Most of the goods were brought from Holland and Belgium, though maybe some were from France. If the smuggling smack had a white mainsail, false numbers were put on with burnt cork and on the bows with white chalk. Approaching the Essex shore they left oyster dredges hanging over the sides to pretend they had been fishing. If the tides were favourable the smuggling smack anchored at the Geeton Creek down the river and filled up the big rowboat they carried. This was rowed quickly up the narrow creek to a farm at South Green, Fingringhoe, where it was landed and hidden for later distribution.

One large Rowhedge smack took part in smuggling for some time. The

Customs men became suspicious and visited the skipper's house. His front room was used for storage of goods but this had been cleared the night before, so it was empty and as the windows were white-washed, it looked as though it was to be papered. All the Customs men could find was a smell of drink and tobacco smoke. Soon after, the smugglers were given away when one of the crew celebrated too freely on board the smack and was later found asleep along the river wall with a bottle of Dutch gin by his side. That put an end to that run of smuggling!

Mrs Harriet Motts lived in Church Lane; Aunt Motts as she was known to almost everyone, young and old, and greatly respected. I can almost see her now, standing perhaps at her front door or talking in the street, her smiling face with spectacles which she wore well down her nose. With respect I would call her a wise woman but a good wise woman. Of course I wasn't very old at the time when Aunt Motts was doing her good deeds in the parish. It seems as if she was gifted with what I would call an inner vision. Her way of life was simple, a cheery smile and a wave as one passed her cottage door, but many there were who sought her advice in health and other matters.

We pass the school, still in use and a place of many memories for generations of Rowhedge children. To most they were the happy days before

Mrs Harriet Motts.

life became more earnest. Close to the upper gate to the school yard was the entrance to the churchyard. Before the early part of this century there were only two places of worship in the village; the parish church of St Lawrence and the Wesleyan Mariners chapel. The church is built in brick and is an unusual eight-sided builting with a pointed slate roof and designed in imitation of the Chapter House at York Cathedral, for reasons unknown to me. It was consecrated in 1838 to replace the old parish church which was a considerable distance out of Rowhedge, although of course inside the parish of East Donyland, along the Fingringhoe road, adjacent to the present Rowhedge cemetery. Some of the seating was in a gallery but most in pews on the ground floor. These were unusually high backed, but certainly suited the interior of the church. Those pews were replaced by chairs several years ago. Lighting was by oil lamps. On each side of the altar there were oblong boards fixed to the wall and painted black with gold lettered words of the Lord's Prayer and the Ten Commandments. Over the top of the altar window were these words: "The earth is the Lord's. The Lord's seat is in heaven," and over the altar itself "Holy, Holy, Holy". On a Sunday morning, if the sun was shining through the window it seemed to throw a lovely gleam over the scene. After the church was built it was found that the window which was a background for the altar, didn't face due east, and I can see it is so. When I was young, the Rector of the parish was the Reverend John Easterling. He was the only person in the church to wear a surplice and no cross was ever carried in procession as it is now. I remember two of the organists of that time; Miss Daniell of Heath House and Mr Pratt. The choir consisted of men and boys and one or two girls; none wore surplices. Services were held on Sunday mornings at 11 a.m.; evenings at 6.30 p.m.; holy baptism on the first Sunday in the month at 3.00 p.m.; and the Good Friday and Christmas Day services were at 11 a.m. The collections on the third Sunday in the month were for church expenses and the first Sunday collection was for the sick and poor. Each following Sunday the amount of collection money for the previous week was always announced.

The church at Easter, Harvest and Christmas was always decorated nicely, but especially so at a Harvest service when, besides the usual flowers, fruit and vegetables, there hung yachts flags, lifebuoys and fishing nets; really it was all most inspiring. This was a service held on a Friday evening before Harvest Thanksgiving, and was always well attended as a thanksgiving for the safe return of sailors of the village from the season's yachting and for the hoped-for-harvest of the sea. For many years now that service has been discontinued at the church.

Further along is Church Hill, a short street leading to a gate to the one end of the present recreation ground, then a field. My uncle, Captain William Cranfield, lived at Yarana House, on Church Hill, named after one of the big racing yachts he had skippered. This house had a monkey puzzle tree in the

My uncles Captain William W. Cranfield, at the tiller, and Captain Lemon Cranfield, standing, racing the America's Cup challenger *Valkyrie II* in 1893. The mate, Mr W. Allen, at extreme right in cheesecutter. The beards make them appear old; Uncle William was then only thirty-seven and Lemon about fifty.

front garden, an object of interest to children, and a tiled path to the front door. Uncle William owned a very fast smack named *Sunbeam*, which was beautifully kept and raced in all the regattas, occasionally beating the swift *Neva*, owned by his brother, Captain Lemon Cranfield. Sometimes, when the yacht *Cariad* was at Rowhedge, her owner, Lord Dunraven, who also owned the America's Cup challengers *Valkyrie II* and *III*, was driven down from Colchester railway station to visit her and would stay at the house of *Cariad's* steward, Mr Teddy Goodrum, who lived next door to my uncle William. What talk of yachting and racing those houses have witnessed!

Further along Church Hill at Marjorie Cottage, lived William's brother, Captain Stephen Cranfield. He had been captain of the yacht *Syren* and mate of the *Valkyrie I*. He owned and sailed the smack *Elizabeth Ann*. At the upper end of Church Hill lived Captain Tom Jay, another famous racing skipper who had sailed the huge racing cutter *Satanita* against the King's *Britannia* with Captain John Carter at the helm, and the *Valkyrie II* raced by William Cranfield, so you see there was great but friendly rivalry between these captains and many others from the same village. Later, Captain Jay skippered the steam yacht *Kempion* whose owner delighted in cruising European and Mediterranean waters for much of the season.

A house named Marina on the corner of the junction of Church Hill with

Captain Tom Jay sailed the 300 ton cutter *Satanita* with a Rowhedge crew. She was the fastest racing cutter ever built, averaging 13.7 knots.

Taylors Road was the last in the village to be named after a yacht — Sir William Burton's 12 metre racer of 1936, in whose crew the owner of the house had sailed. This custom died out in 1939 when all the yachts laid up on the outbreak of War, after which big yachting never restarted. However, I feel it is a pity that some Rowhedge houses which were named for famous yachts whose prize money had financed their building, have had these proud names removed by later owners who probably often did not know the origin and reason for the names. How nice it would be if new owners were to learn the story behind the house name and perhaps decide to keep it when they knew the history of the yacht it commemorates. Probably a picture of the yacht would be available and could be hung in the house, as sailing pictures are again fashionable.

On the subject of house names, there was one in Taylors Road which always intrigued me; in earlier times it had been a public house called *The Apple Tree* and in later years, when it had become a private house, it was unusually named Envied Industry. However, that is taken down now and the property has become two houses. If we go back along Church Hill and enter Regent Street, the first houses on the right are Valkyrie Cottages, one of which I own and live in. My mother's brother, Captain William Cranfield, had them built in 1895. Good solid houses; all the timber in them is in as good a condition as the day they were built, at least I can say this of the one I live in. It is said that my uncle paid a man £100 just to keep an eye on their construction while he was away in America as captain of the *Valkyrie III* racing for the America's Cup. Practically opposite are four houses which Captain Isiah Powell of the *Sunbeam* had built in 1899, when he had become captain of the large steam yacht *Sunflower*, hence the name of the houses.

Lower down Regent Street my brother, James Barnard, had a house built in 1913. As a boy Jim went to sea fishing in our father's smack before going as a hand in yachts and eventually becoming one of a racing crew, which was the ambition of most young men at Rowhedge at that time. You see, hands in racing yachts had to be the very smartest of sailors, which made them proud to be picked for such a crew and they earned better money than most men in cruising yachts, besides getting a share in the prize money which the yacht won each season, and which could amount to a considerable sum in the values of the time. As a young man Jim was one of the crew of the huge America's Cup challenger *Valkyrie III*, her captain, William Cranfield, and his crew of 37 were almost all Rowhedge men. As at the same time many other very large racing and cruising yachts were captained and crewed by men from the village, you can realise how important yachting was to Rowhedge and also to Wivenhoe and Brightlingsea, which were the three places where most of the local racing yachtsmen came from until Tollesbury and West Mersea men were brought into it, mostly as hands.

110

Uncle William was also captain of the huge racing cutter *Valkyrie III*, which raced for the America's Cup during 1895, with a crew of forty, who were almost all Rowhedge men. She was 187 feet from the end of the bowsprit to the end of the boom and set 13,000 square feet of canvas, without the spinnaker.

At first Jim rose to be skipper of some attractive small yachts including the sleek little *Onaway* whose owner was so pleased with her performance with Jim as skipper that when he left England to live abroad he presented Jim with the yacht! Later on my brother became captain of quite large sailing yachts, such as the 15 metre *Cestrian*, the 100 ton yawl *Rendesvous* and the 12 metre

Iyruna. Early in the 1920s Jim thought his luck had gone when the owner of the yacht which he then skippered decided to sell her in more or less mid-season, and the new owner already had his own skipper and crew, which seemed a catastrophe for my brother. However, as luck would have it, it turned out to be the opposite.

After calling to see us at my father's home one afternoon and bemoaning his fate, Jim said he would have a walk down on the ferry-yard. It was a lovely afternoon and he hadn't been down there long when he recognised someone coming over in the ferry boat. It was no less than Sir William Burton, the noted racing yacht owner. My brother greeted him saying, "Good afternoon Sir William," and he replied, "Why, it's not you Jim, is it? At home at midsummer!" They had a talk together and Sir William went on to explain why he was in Rowhedge on that day and asked my brother if he knew of a hand who would join his yacht almost at once, because a man was leaving who was nervous of the risks while racing. Jim quickly thought it out and knowing that he stood no foreseeable chance of becoming captain of any yacht so late that year, he made his decision on the spot and told Sir William that he would take the vacant berth on his yacht for the remainder of the season. So Sir William's journey was not in vain, nor was my brother's decision without its reward, for the next season, when Captain Albert Turner left Sir William to take command of the King's racing yacht *Britannia*, Sir William made my brother Jim captain of his yacht. After he had got beyond the years of yacht racing, Sir William had the fine diesel yacht *Caleta* built by Phillips of Dartmouth with Jim also as her captain. The yacht came to lay up at Rowhedge each winter in

My brother Jim's last command was the 138 ton motor yacht *Caleta*, owned by Sir William Burton.

Rook Bay and my brother stayed with Sir William until he retired from yachting when war started in 1939. Jim also retired at the same time, ending a partnership under the red, white and black Burton racing flag.

Almost opposite Jim's house lived Captain Jesse Cranfield and his wife and family. This particular family of Cranfields were no relation to me, having originated from West Mersea, but they were always my "uncle and aunt" just the same. Jesse Cranfield captained several racing yachts including the large and beautiful schooner *Cicely* and the black yawl *Merrythought*. Come to think of it, Regent Street should have been named Captains Road as Captains A. Wilkin, J. Simons, C. Simons and Richard Cranfield were also living here.

About half way down the Street is the Methodist Church, built in 1913 for a faithful band of worshippers who since 1910 had been content to hold their services in a small outhouse belonging to the bakery which was opposite the Lion Hall. What joy it must have brought to them when they attended the very first service at their new church, their hopes realised; and each of them remained faithful until their life's end.

I am indebted to Mr Jack Wilkin for the following details of the Rowhedge Methodist Church, from the Golden Jubilee year booklet 1913-1963. It states that it owes its origin to Mr Jonathan Payne Watcham of Great Bentley, who came to Rowhedge, later to become manager of Stacey Wood's grocery shop. It was a deeply religious and conscientious young man who came to the village to marry Jane Carter, a local girl from a well-known Rowhedge family. She eventually became Aunt Jane to all who knew her, and a good hearted Aunt Jane she was too.

When first arriving in the village Mr Watcham attended the Parish Church and then the Mariners Chapel. From the days of his youth he had been a Primitive Methodist. Eventually he proposed to the Mariners Chapel that they amalgamate, but the proposition didn't meet with success. So in 1910 John Watcham, together with his brother-in-law Mr James Benson, also a "pillar of the Church", started to convert the small building into a place of worship and, when they had completed their labour of love, they commenced to hold services there, conducted with dignity and reverence. A choir was formed, and its members contributed 3d per week which helped towards the new building funds. Many public teas were held to contribute to this, together with gifts from the worshippers of the Church.

Eventually, on Whit Monday, 1913, the foundation stones of the Rowhedge Methodist Church were laid, and the ceremony I understand was informal and the weather very kind. Gathered there were a bearded and frock coated cleric, and fashionably dressed ladies of the congregation, husbands and families. When the new church was completed and ready for the Dedication, the clerics and congregation assembled outside and by the invitation of the Reverend Watson-Grayson, the Reverend J. Harper then came forward, and on opening the Church door said: "To the Glory of God and in the Name of the Father, Son and Holy Ghost." Ministers and people then entered the Church for the remainder of the Dedication Service.

At the opening Mr James Taylor became Chapel Steward, and his wife became its first organist. Mr I. J. Aldridge became the first Superintendent of the Chapel Sunday School. The original members of the congregation are no more, but the enthusiasm is still there, carried on by their descendants. The Chapel Stewardship today is held by Mr L. Benson, a son of Mr James Benson, one of the founders of the Church. Today's organist is Mrs M. Hillyard, daughter of Mr and Mrs W. Turff, both of whom were also founder members. Mr Derek Marshall is today's Sunday School Superintendent with great interest in the work it entails. The services there are sincere and bright and above all there is a warm welcome awaiting everyone who enters. Inside it is very pleasant, well decorated, carpeted and warm. The Sunday School has a large number of scholars and sometimes on occasions like prize giving they assist during the service by reading the lessons. Now that the Parish Church at Harvest Festival has discontinued its Friday evening thanksgiving service for sailors' safe return, and for the Harvest of the Sea, a very similar service is held in the Methodist Church and from time to time a talk is given by a representative of the Missions to Seamen.

The ladies sewing party is thriving and one only has to go to the Church's annual bazaar to see the results of their labours. The bazaar is held a few weeks before Christmas in the pavilion, and the building gets really full of people, waiting to buy the goods on sale. Recently it was practically impossible for people to get anywhere near the counters. I saw garments passed over peoples' heads to those unable to get near the counters, sending the money up the same way, so eager were the people to buy. Well, they all know good value is always given whether it is for garments, confectionery, or fancy goods. Practically everything on offer is sold and very quickly. For several years now the takings at the bazaar have amounted to well over £200 annually.

The Church has quite recently been thoroughly redecorated and carpeted and the seating arrangements slightly altered, and with the individual gifts from many of its members, they have really beautified it. Long may it flourish.

Further down Regent Street was Rowhedge's largest shop, the Co-op grocery and butcher's departments, in a spacious building, still thriving to-day. On the opposite side of the road was the brick built Lion Hall behind *The White Lion* public house. The Hall was used for concerts and other public events including wedding receptions and launching dinners but was demolished a few years ago, when houses were built on the site.

We have now reached the lower end of Regent Street where it joins the High Street, with the public open space opposite, which was once part of the Shipyard and earlier the public hard of "No Man's Land".

CHAPTER SEVEN

Family, Food and Fashion

MUCH has been written from time to time of the men of Rowhedge, their seafaring and shipbuilding, so here I would like to try to convey to you my early memories of the women of the village, of their homes and their great love for their families. To their memory I would pay tribute to their faithfulness, cleanliness and tidiness in the way they kept their homes, almost without exception. In those days there were no gadgets to lessen the hard work of keeping their houses so spick and span; the only soap powder was "Watson's Matchless Cleaner", "Fels naptha soap", Brown Windsor, and later Lifebuoy and Sunlight. Hot water systems in houses were unheard of. It was necessary to fetch water from the brook, water wells and the pumps at the top of Parkfield, until the piped water was laid on; even then very few houses had water indoors and the tap was outside, near the back door. Not many had a mangle either, so most of them took their linen and mangled it in an outhouse in Dark House Lane, where a Mrs Simons lived and where one could mangle a whole basket of linen for a payment of 1d or 1½d. But the mangle that I remember most was in the garden outhouse of one of our neighbours. It was so unusual, being about 9 to 10 feet long, with an iron wheel and iron handle and was like a huge oblong wooden box weighted with large stones. There were two rollers, one on each side of the wheel which had a linen cloth attached, and on these cloths the garments were laid in position, first one side of the wheel and then the other. One would start to turn the wheel and the box-like top would go backwards and forwards. The result was clothes beautifully mangled, but it was hard work turning that wheel, I can tell you. Until quite recently there was a mangle exactly like this in the Colchester Castle Museum, but the Rowhedge one was made from beautiful wood, oak I suppose, which seemed highly polished and even the rollers looked as if they had been polished too. It was certainly a museum piece although I cannot possibly guess its age. Needless to say that it was dismantled several years ago.

I also remember all the starching and ironing that went on in those days, as almost all girls went to school in very nice white pinafores over their dresses. Some would have a pretty bow of either pink or blue ribbon on the left side of the chest. Then there were the white cotton underskirts edged with embroidery flounces, and the white silk and embroidery dresses that many children wore in summer time, all stiff and starched. All this and no electric irons, but by box iron or a heated ordinary flat iron. Oh yes, ironing took up a great deal of time but those women were never daunted; the lovely white lace curtains at their windows bore out that fact.

There was at most a mere handful of six-roomed houses in the village until the very late 1890s, and some had sculleries attached. In these, food was usually eaten in the kitchen, and at week-ends perhaps in the second downstairs room, which was called the "keeping room". "Keeping room" is a term which is also to be found in books on Suffolk. The front room was kept and used only on high days and at Christmas. With the building of six-roomed houses came the kitchener stoves with ovens; before that people cooked on open stoves with a hob each side, the rest of the cooking being taken to the two village bakeries; Ladbrooke's and Amos's. A large proportion of the villagers took their dinners to the bakeries to be cooked for 1d on weekdays, 1½d on Sundays and cakes on Saturday afternoons. I can see now the lines of baking tins lying on top of flour troughs in the bakehouse waiting to go into the oven. All dinners had to be there by 11 a.m. There would be Yorkshire puddings and joints of beef etc, some in partitioned tins. As I have already said, looking back it still remains a mystery to me how those varied dishes were all baked to a turn. The dinners were ready by one o'clock for all to collect and I never ever heard of one dinner not cooked properly. After the washing is done and the dinners cooked, now of the women themselves. They were faithful wives and loving mothers and great love existed between parents and children, who always knew that their mothers would be at home when they came home from school. In fact, the mother of the family, if her husband went to sea as most men did, was alone responsible for her children's upbringing for the greater part of each year.

Wives endured a lot of anxiety when in the winter many men went stowboating for sprats in the smacks; on one such winter's night when a gale was raging, one mother I know gathered her four children around her and told them to kneel with her and pray that their father would be kept safe at sea in the gale. That father was my eldest brother, and the mother was his wife, my sister Margie, my sister-in-law really, but we in our family always spoke of our sisters-in-law as our sisters. Neighbours were very kind to one another and we would call nearly everyone Aunt and Uncle. I had many related aunts and uncles and those that were not we would address as "my uncle" or "my aunt" followed by their surname. Two in particular I remember with affection; they both lived in Regent Street but have passed on these many years and lives are the poorer for their passing; they were always ready to give a helping hand to one and all.

The mothers also saw that their children attended Sunday School. A great many had a round table in the centre of their sitting-room and in the centre of this you would see the family Bible surrounded by Sunday School prize books which their children had been given. On Sunday evenings they would read to

Housewives enjoying afternoon tea. My sister-in-law Margie Barnard at left.

the family from the family Bible if they hadn't been to Church or Chapel. In my case it was my father who read to me as my mother had died, and on one such occasion I can still remember hearing the tolling of the Church bell as we turned over the leaves of the Bible because I wanted to see the really lovely coloured pictures it contained. Such memories die hard, indeed they have become "golden memories".

Shopping in Colchester was a rarity in those days, about three or four visits a year by the majority of women, when they went to buy clothes and footwear for themselves and their children. Although unnecessary outings were not often made I have no doubt that some occasionally travelled farther afield as did one village woman who spent a short holiday in London. When she arrived back home, someone asked her how she had enjoyed her stay, and she replied "To much 'whiff waff' for me; give me good old England." Well, really, what do you make of it? Her reply became quite a saying in the village, ridiculed of course.

Dresses and coats were worn very long and most women of middle-age favoured black, navy blue or grey for colour. Dresses had fairly tight fitting bodices and very full skirts with wide tucks at the hem, frills or flounces. The bodice would be tucked too and many had bead trimmings. The neck line was

117

A village housewife in her best.

My sister Hettie during 1914, in typical best clothes of the time.

very high and was boned, and more often than not had a tiny lace edging at the top to finish it off. Other bodices would have a deep lined lace yoke and collar and bishop sleeves were very much favoured, although as an alternative leg-of-mutton sleeves were worn, very wide at the shoulder and tight at the wrist. Feather boas were much worn on summer evenings and looked very nice too, I thought, especially those that were brown and white.

Hats for summer wear were in the main of voile or chiffon or a mixture of both. Some were toques,* others larger versions of the toque which seemed to be about four inches high, with either a spray of osprey or ostrich feathers. many wore bonnets, making the wearers look much older than their years. In winter, hats were made of felt or velour, many decorated with birds in the front on the top of the crown.

In the cold days of winter many wore popular costumes of thick cloth. I remember about that time Miss Frances Robinson, who was organist at our Sunday School, wore such a costume, mole shade, with a three quarter length coat; her hat was of amethyst colour velour and together with her sable furs and her regal figure, she looked very smart indeed; yes even now I remember how I saw it all about sixty-five years ago.

As young children, we too liked to have pretty clothes. The prevailing fashions for us in summer were cream serge dresses with white silk embroidery and kilts made of serge, in navy blue or cream. Hats for us were usually leghorn‡ or satin straw, rather large and wide brimmed, some trimmed with bows of satin, a row of daisies and buttercups or pink rosebuds around the crown. Others would be trimmed with ostrich feathers of pure white. I took a pride in the ostrich feathers I wore, beautifully curled, as my eldest brother George had brought them home from South Africa, he at that time being a ship's carpenter on various ships of the Union Castle line. I always felt mine were better than anyone else's, but there was a snag in the wearing of ostrich feathers. Like so many people in Rowhedge we nearly always went to church or chapel on Sunday evenings, and after the service we would go for a walk on a summer evening, either up to the heath or along the river wall. We were all right, or should I say the ostrich feathers were, until the "Da ag" or mist started to rise. To combat this, we usually took a large handkerchief which we put over the feathers in an effort to prevent them from coming out of curl and then we hurried home as quickly as we could. This was a common sight, for the "'Da ag", as you may know, soon changed the temperature, and in fact it did much more than that. One theory was that it caused some diseases and ill health. I suppose when one is born and bred in an area one gets acclimatised to it, but that "Da ag" still comes and rises from the marshes on hot summer evenings and it tells some of us that the morrow will be a lovely day. Its name is supposed to be of Danish origin.

Now I will turn to the teenagers and some a bit older. They too liked their

*A small, brimless, close fitting bonnet.
‡A plait of straw of bearded wheat cut green and bleached (originally imported from Leghorn) — thus a bonnet or hat made of this plait.

pretty clothes, more or less in the style worn by the older people, but of course not so long — about mid calf length. For best summer wear they would choose to have their dresses made in materials of either cashmere, heavy georgette, silk, sometimes satin, and flowered voile, mostly in pastel shades and lovely too. Crease-resisting materials were unheard of but that was overcome by frequent ironing. Navy blue or navy blue and white striped costumes were much worn; cream costumes too and cream serge pleated skirts and shirt blouses. When winter came, of course they had winter coats and costumes with coats which were much longer than some of today's suits. Shoes were usually of the button-up style until court shoes were worn or patent leather with large buckles. Winter shoes were far stouter than are worn today and again the button-up style prevailed and older women wore them with elastic sides.

As everyone wore a hat in those days one can imagine their great variety. Some were made by a milliner in Rowhedge, others by Miss Jennings who kept a shop in Short Wyre Street, Colchester; and of course some were bought from other shops. On the whole hats tended to be quite large, Leghorn tagee straw was everyone's dream hat, usually in black with lovely shaded silk roses complete with foliage circling the crown, and the brims of the hats were very wide. Then there were Dolly Vardon hats; usually the wearers looked very attractive in them; and hats of lace and tulle and, later, came the sunshine hats; a grown-up version of children's poke bonnets, and straw sailor hats too. Winter hats were usually of felt or velour and of course with them almost everyone wore furs and carried muffs. Some muffs even had purses let into them. Gloves were worn; usually for winter it was kid gloves and for summer white fabric. Lace mitts were also worn by some.

The trend for most men was to wear navy blue suits for best, whether they were seafaring or not. Of course the sailors always did as they were fitted out in these each year at the yacht owner's expense.

Small boys in the early 1900s often wore white sailor suits and as they grew older ordinary boy's suits. Some had Norfolk style jackets. As boys will be boys they mostly wore sturdy shoes and boots, but often when summer came they wore black or brown canvas shoes which took quite a heavy sole. Of course nearly every child had a new pair of plimsolls for the Sunday School treats, thinking they could run better in them. But what pleased many boys was to wear one of their father's jerseys with the name of the yacht he was in and initials of her yacht club embroidered on the front. Many wore them for school and were very proud of them, particularly if the name was of a famous racing yacht, as they often were, and even more so if it also had the initials "R.Y.S." standing for the Royal Yacht Squadron underneath.

CHAPTER EIGHT

Chapel Street and Transport

CHAPEL Street is the only street in the village that I have yet to comment on. Many of the old cottages were demolished years ago, and attractive new properties have taken their places. However, the Weslyan Mariners Chapel is still there and its band of worshippers are as devoted to it as were those of days gone by. The congregation is much smaller, but wasn't it our Lord Himself who said "Where one or two are gathered together in My Name, there am I in the midst of them"?

Appropriately enough, the Mariners Chapel was built by a shipwright; Mr John Martin, a Rowhedge man who then lived at the Hythe, the port of Colchester, up the river. By the 1850s he had risen to become foreman of the shipyard owned by J. Mann, on the site where Brown's timber wharf now stands. This yard built many wooden square-rigged sailing ships and other craft. When the Mariners Chapel was finished, Mr Martin and his wife used to walk to Rowhedge and back for the services.

Later it was administered by the Scrutton family and it remained so up to about 1970. I would like to pay tribute to this family for their untiring devotion to the Chapel and to its members and to the Sunday School. If I could single one out it would be Mr Harold Scrutton, originally a yacht decorator. Never daunted, he gave lifelong service and to this day is remembered with affection among his congregation, young and old alike. His daughter, Mrs I. Brown, carries on the work her father did before her, following in his footsteps and, she like him, is strong in the Faith. Mrs Brown is the last of the Scrutton family living in Rowhedge.

The services at the Chapel have always been very bright and the singing beautiful. At anniversary times and at the Service of Song which was held occasionally during winter time, the singing was greatly enjoyed, for they had at that time a large choir with remarkable harmonizing from the men's voices. Young men of the Wilkin and Hilliard families were great singers and the voice of Mr Jack Wilkin still enriches the service whenever he sings.

Magic Lantern shows were held in the Chapel schoolroom at intervals during winter and were much enjoyed, in spite of the lantern often breaking down or the slides occasionally appearing upside down!

The congregation in those days was very large, especially when the men came home from yachting in the autumn, as many of them and their families had their own seats in the Chapel and their children were scholars of the

121

Sunday School. Now the Chapel has been taken over by the Datchet Evangelical Trust, but Mrs Brown is still most active in all the services held there, and as Superintendent of the Sunday School always extends a great welcome to everyone.

Adjoining the Chapel to the north, are two cottages now in the process of being restored, the further one was in years gone by occupied by my aunt and uncle Cudmore, with their family. Both cottages were four-roomed, but the one my aunt lived in had a kitchen built on, one wall of which went nearly up to the roof of the cottage and on this wall was slung a full size penny farthing bicycle belonging to George, one of their sons; a very queer thing to be slung from a wall you will say, but it is perfectly true and I have walked under it many times when going from living room to kitchen.

Next is Olive House, once the home of the Scrutton family. A much larger house of course; eight rooms and bathroom. This house has been thoroughly modernized and I thought it extremely comfortable and so tastefully furnished when I was shown over it recently by its new owners, after enjoying afternoon tea with them. Just across the road is the brick building and yard where Mr Ben Harris stabled his horse and carrier's van which plied between Colchester and Rowhedge.

Almost at the end of Chapel Street we stand on the spot where the gate into Rowhedge stood, although no sign of it remains today as the last of its posts was removed about two years ago when access to the brook was boarded up. There is a sadness to my mind in all these changes, however small.

However, the little brook still gurgles under the road at the bottom of Town Fields Hill, today known as Rowhedge Road, and it is now a very busy road. I cannot remember the actual gate at the bottom of Chapel Street, but have seen the old gate posts in position. Evidently this gate was open from early morning until the carrier had finished his rounds when, not too late at night, he would close and lock it until morning came. So there was then only one alternative entry into Rowhedge which was by taking the Fingringhoe Road at Old Heath and forking off to the left at *The Ipswich Arms*, walking on to Rowhedge from there. At night Rowhedge was then a more or less closed village, until the new road was constructed, to the left of Chapel Street, running from the brook to Marsh Stile Gate, linking up with the High Street. This New Road, as it came to be called, was built by the Army early in this century and is now known as Marsh Crescent.

In years gone by there was also a Toll Gate by the house known as Cleavelands, up the Town Fields, which I have heard about from two people, and two years ago Mr J. Theobald, then ninety-two years old, told me that it was quite elaborate in design and had an appropriate verse carved on it:

"Welcome all who freely pay
a trifle for repairs;

both good and bad can pass this way,
      the wheat, also the tares.
All ye who on the cycle ride,
must pass at ebb and flow of tide;
although without a horse you travel,
your flying wheels disturb the gravel."

This Toll Gate appears on the original deeds of land in Rowhedge Road, which are the property of my nephew-in-law, Mr Wilfred Ainger, so Cleavelands was the Toll Gate house and a toll was levied on vehicles entering or leaving Rowhedge, to pay for road maintenance.

Transport in the early 1900s was, for nearly everyone, by "Shanks Pony" and the villagers walked the lanes, paths and roadways for miles and thought nothing of walking in to Colchester and back to do some shopping. It was always considered by us to be three miles from Rowhedge to the Camp Church, in Military Road, Colchester, and that we were half-way to Colchester when we got to Cuddon's Brewery at Old Heath.

At the foot of the little hill after passing the Old Heath Bell, there was a stream. Nearby, water flowed out of a pipe which jutted out from a small bricked pillar. On a summer's afternoon, having become rather warm walking, many would put their hands together and catch the water from this pipe and drink it. Friends and I have done this many a time and have found the water most refreshing. It was as it were a "wayfarers' fountain". After this brief halt it was on to Colchester again. Nearing Whitehall, a large house which had extensive grounds, was a section of the main road where the trees met overhead and offered shelter to the walker against sun and rain. It was here that one could see the peacocks strutting the grass or calling from the branches of trees. Now and then some could be seen with their wings and tail outstretched, a pretty sight indeed, their tails posed in the shape of a fan. Of course when the peacock calls, it's a sign of rain, everyone said. Needless to say Whitehall was demolished years ago and with it went the avenue of trees. Since early in the 1900s or before, a great many houses have been built on its meadows, and for years now the whole estate has been built up entirely as part of the district of Colchester known as Old Heath.

Continuing our walk into Colchester we still had Digby's Hill to climb. Then it was not far to the Recreation Ground and Camp Church, and along Military Road into the town to any shops we needed to visit. If we stayed a little later, especially in the winter time, we always liked to see other people we knew walking home, as it got dark earlier under the avenue of trees at Whitehall. Also, when we were approaching Rans Lane, which was on the town side of Cleavelands, we always put on an extra spurt as we felt a sense of nervousness going through the Lane; all girls did anyway. I remember walking home from town one evening with an old friend of mine, Celia Fale, and when we were half way home it suddenly became very overcast at Abbots Road. Within minutes quite a gale blew up and it rained in torrents. We were still about quarter of an hour's walk away from Rans Lane and oh dear, we were scared but consoled ourselves by saying that nobody would chase us on a night such as this. Eventually we arrived home safe and sound but wet through.

Of course there were some who owned horses and traps in Rowhedge, including Mr Robert Pearson, the yacht painter, Mr Alf Everitt the shoemaker and Mr Enos Harris of the yachtbuilding firm. His was a Victorian design, low on the ground, with high wheels in which his nephew Sidney Walford used to drive him about.

Mr W. Carter also had a horse and trap and on one occasion the horse shied and threw him out of it. The story goes that when Aunt Motts saw him afterwards, she joked with him about it, and lifting her arm and waving it in a good-natured manner, she said "Ah, ah, Buddy Boy. I told you that Old Hoss 'oud"! Her comment was in the good old Essex style.

Dr Kevern also had a horse and trap and often used it when on visits to his sick patients. Sometimes he drove it himself, otherwise Lewis Powell, whom the doctor employed, would have the reins. The Reverend Mr Easterling, Rector of our Parish Church, was the owner of a pony and governess cart in which he often drove his family into Colchester. Once when I was walking home from Colchester, they stopped and offered me a lift which I accepted with thanks.

Mr Ben Harris and Mr Edgar Jones were the two village carriers with horses and vans and their stables still stand to this day; Mr Jones' at the back of the house that he lived in at Church Hill and Mr Harris's still to be seen in Chapel Street, but for how much longer is anyone's guess, as the land it stands on went up for auction recently.

Mr Harris had been a very smart racing yachtsman and became skipper of several smaller racing yachts during the 1870s-1880s. I believe that by 1889 he had risen to be captain of the ten ton class yacht *Queen Mab*, with which he and his village crew were very successful all round the British coasts. The last race of that season was at Torbay regatta in rough weather and this cast a shadow over Captain Harris's life because, during it, while the *Queen Mab* was leading, her bowsprit broke off and the mast and clouds of canvas were carried away and fell aft on to Captain Harris at the tiller and a guest sitting by him, seriously injuring both. So Captain Harris came ashore for good and buying himself a horse and van became a carrier from Rowhedge. How he must have longed for salt water and the helm of a racing yacht as he jogged back and forth to Colchester. He charged 3d for a single fare and would also shop in Colchester for anyone, charging 2d per call at a shop or for a parcel collected. I have journeyed to Colchester in both carriers' vans and I suppose each one would hold at most from eight to ten people. I remember my sister Hettie and

124

I went to town by Mr Jones' van one morning, and he had to make a call at Cleavelands. He seemed to be there quite a time on his business. The horse got restless and started off at a slow trot. Hettie and I looked at each other and didn't know how to stop it, so we took the reins and pulled them back as tight as ever we could, and we stopped it just about where Battlesbrook Road is today. Of course the horse wasn't capable of much speed, but we didn't enjoy the experience any the more. Mr Jones soon came hurrying up behind and caught us up, so all was well for the remainder of the journey.

An alternative way of getting to Colchester if one didn't want to use the carrier or walk it, was by way of the ferry, and then by train from Wivenhoe to St Botolph's Station. The railway fare was 3½d single, and the ferry charge was ½d from 6 a.m. onwards until 9 p.m. when it became 1d and 2d after 10 p.m. Officially the ferry closed at 10 p.m. but it had to overrun its time by a few minutes to wait for any passengers who might have alighted off the last London train at Wivenhoe, and wanted to go to Rowhedge. They had to walk to the ferry along the gravel path across the marsh, now shut and swallowed up by a timber yard.

In 1919 motor buses started to run between Colchester and Rowhedge. The service was started by Berry and Sons of Port Lane, Colchester. The fare was 3d single or 5d return. The price of the return ticket dropped when the Primrose Bus Company of Mersea Island started up in opposition. As you can imagine the people of the village thought it grand to be able to get into town by bus, the price being so reasonable too, but even then many continued to walk it, for after all 3d was 3d in those days, and at that time the girls who worked at the Rowhedge clothing factory (of which I was one) only received a wage of 2/6d each week when they first started.

After the buses had been running a few months, Berry's put a new charabanc "The Dorothy" on the run and this caused quite a stir, everyone wanting to get into the back seats, which were built up in tier style, making them much higher than the front ones. As far as I remember this vehicle was open to wind and weather, so all the girls' hair got ruffled on the journey, but who cared; hair perms were unheard of in those days. When departure time came the charabanc would vacate its stand outside *The Albion Hotel*, Colchester bound. After a time Berry's extended their service to and from the nearby village of Fingringhoe, which was greatly appreciated by the villagers as almost none had cars in those days. The Primrose Bus Company didn't operate very long from Rowhedge, but in its place emerged two others, one operated by Mr Tom Fale. What a jovial character was he, with his happy smile and friendly greeting to one and all who knew him, which did one good to behold. He went to sea in his earlier life as steward or cook in yachts, and was one of the crew of the *Valkyries* when they raced for the America's Cup, but he gave up going to sea and while living in Taylors Road, at the house called Envied Industry (certainly he never gave the house its name) started a fish and chip business there. Prices were fried fish from 1d per piece and chips ½d and how beautifully cooked they were. After a few years he vacated the premises and set up again in the fried fish business in the High Street, near where I lived. Of course this was all before 1914. After a few years in the High Street he changed his way of business and re-opened the shop as a general shop selling sweets and on Saturday afternoons made and sold ice cream. Cornets were ½d each, but sometimes would-be customers waiting to buy one were disappointed, as the machine that made the ice cream had a habit of breaking down just at a vital moment. However, the shop carried on in the sweets and grocery line and during this time Mr Fale acquired the carrier business of Mr Ben Harris. He continued to run it on exactly the same lines as Mr Harris, also taking tailoring to the Colchester Manufacturing Company and Hollingtons Clothing Factories, as many women of the village did tailoring in their homes and sent in their bundles of finished garments, usually on Thursday or Friday. When their work had been passed, they were sent another bundle to make up and received payment for work done; all via the carrier and I believe all this was executed for only 4d expense to the workers.

His daughter Celia Fale was one of my old friends from school days. In the playground she kept us all in order, and lined us up against the brick wall if anyone had over-stepped it during playtime. Oh, it was all in fun, we all enjoyed it and called her "policeman". Celia became Mrs Maudesley and retained her robust nature over the years, the smiles were always there. When I heard that she had passed away at Christmas 1972, I must confess it was quite a blow to me. Always remaining friends through the years and always being greeted so cordially, it became a treat to meet her.

Later, Fale's carriers' cart was replaced by a bus and Fale's very efficient bus service existed into the 1960s, when it was bought by the Eastern National Company and added to their route. The other Rowhedge bus was run by Mr Charles Warner, who gave up during the 1940s.

CHAPTER NINE

The Great War

ALTHOUGH most people did not realise it, the start of the War in 1914 ended an era in their lives. Young and middle-aged men volunteered for the army in hundreds of thousands and marched off to die in the mud and horror of the French battlefields. Naturally, many Rowhedge men served in the Royal Navy, the Royal Naval Reserve, and the Volunteer Reserve, on the seas of the world. Others served in merchant ships, with equal courage, and a few in the early aeroplanes. Many never returned from what was perhaps the greatest tragic war ever known, when a generation was lost to win a peace which was later thrown away. Certainly this country has never fully recovered from the results of the First World War; although it now seems far away, I believe its effects are still with us.

Early in the war it was thought that the Germans might attempt to invade England by landing on the Essex coast and a considerable number of troops were stationed in the area, besides the large garrison at Colchester. Many were billeted in Wivenhoe, Rowhedge and other surrounding villages, and the local population had instructions to evacuate to Messing, inland, if a landing took place. Although this was all very frightening, of course nothing of the sort happened.

Early on a fine spring morning in 1915 we could hear considerable activity over at Wivenhoe. The tramp of marching troops and shouted orders echoed near the railway station, where a puffing train awaited to take them for embarkation in troopships, perhaps at Southampton. As the mists of early morning hung over the marshes and the stars paled, we could hear them singing before the train pulled out. They were bound for the landings in Gallipoli, to fight the Turks and Germans at the Dardanelles.

At the beginning of the war the Royal Engineers built a wooden trestle bridge over the river Colne at Rowhedge, crossing from Pearson's Quay to Wivenhoe wall and enabling troops and guns to be transferred from one side of the river to the other, without having to go round via Colchester. The bridge had a gap about 50 feet wide in its middle which could be filled in, but which stood open most of the time to let smacks, sailing barges and steamboats pass through to Rowhedge upper quays and to Colchester Hythe. For some reason the Army insisted that all craft which passed through did so stern first. Often the sailing barges had to get through with ropes on to buoys above and

A sailing barge with bowsprit topped up prepares to drop down through the opening in the army bridge across the Colne, connecting Rowhedge with Wivenhoe marsh. This was built by the Royal Engineers during the 1914-18 war but was demolished soon after. Barges then wore red ensigns for identification by patrol vessels.

below the bridge, which was greatly disliked by all seafaring people, although it was obviously necessary.

One day in April 1916 there was great excitement in Rowhedge and Wivenhoe; the King was coming! He was inspecting troops of the Southern Army at Clacton during the morning and in the afternoon he passed through Wivenhoe in an open car, down the High Street and Station Road, through the toll gate and across the road to Rowhedge ferry hard, where he alighted. The route was lined with soldiers and hundreds of people. King George V looked dignified in Army uniform and cheerfully acknowledged the cheers. Escorted by Field Marshal Sir John French and other officers and aides the King then formally opened the bridge and walked across it. A car was waiting on the Rowhedge side but the King decided to see for himself the little village where the captain and crew of his racing yacht came from, walking up the High Street between cheering people before boarding his car and being driven off to London.

Air raid warnings were given in towns. In Colchester at such times the trams had large boards placed on their fronts with "Air Raid" on them in big letters. I suppose alerts were given from coast watchers who had seen some Gotha type aeroplanes, as the most frequent German raiders were called, crossing the coast.

One day whilst visiting Clacton in the summertime, seven Gothas approached the coast and were fired on by guns along the shore and by several destroyers steaming along the coast from Harwich, keeping up their firing and pursuit past Colne Point. The shells burst with puffs in the sky but apparently did not hit the raiders. It was very frightening. The gunboat, H.M.S. *Cockchafer*, which was stationed in the mouth of the river Colne as guardship, came out and started firing at them with her guns, so altogether it was quite an affair and we went home feeling very excited but thankful it all ended as it did. The aeroplanes went off and we read next day that seven Gothas had been brought down either on their way to bomb London or on the return home.

The greatest local air activity was when the German Zeppelin L.33 met its fate on Saturday night, 23rd September 1916. Evidently after it had released its bombs much further inland, it made for the Essex coast and headed for the North Sea and home, so the Germans hoped, but this was not to be. In the middle of that night the villagers of the tiny hamlet of Little Wigborough were awakened from their sleep by the roar of the 700 feet long Zeppelin's engines flying low over them, out towards the river Blackwater. I suppose the villagers were feeling thankful that at least it had gone, but after a very short while the Zeppelin returned and landed in a field just behind the two cottages at Little Wigborough. I believe it had been hit earlier in the night, for it was on fire as it landed, although rumour had it that it been fired by the Germans

In September 1916 the 700 feet long German Zeppelin L.33 crashed at the tiny rural village of Little Wigborough, about seven miles from Rowhedge, and was burned out. The huge skeleton, close to the cottages in the background, drew spectators from miles around.

themselves. It was a remarkable escape for the occupants of the cottages and had the wind been in the opposite direction they would most certainly have been enveloped in flames, the Zeppelin being so close, only a matter of a few yards. Of course the people were terrified and hid in their cupboards. I cannot say whether the Germans knocked on their doors or not, nevertheless for those people in the two cottages it was a terrible ordeal. However, the Germans soon left the scene of their burnt-out Zeppelin, walked the two lanes that led to the Peldon Road and gave themselves up to a village policeman. Later they were taken to West Mersea and were locked in a barn before being taken to Colchester. That same night there was born in Wigborough a baby girl who was named and christened "Zeppelina".

The events of the night were exciting but when morning came Little Wigborough had never seen the likes of it before or since. All roads leading in that direction were as crowded as I imagine Epsom district would be on Derby Day. Crowds everywhere, all anxious to see the burnt-out shell of the Zeppelin. There were people in their hundreds; cyclists, people driving in horses and carts, in anything that had wheels, and crowds came on "Shanks Pony". And that is how I arrived there with my sister Hettie and Louise Gredley. We went down the lanes to Little Wigborough to view the phenomenon, but it was so well guarded by the men of the Lancashire Fusiliers that no one could get near it. So after a rest or two by the roadside we made for home at Rowhedge, which was roughly 7 miles away. However we evidently hadn't seen enough of it because on the next day we three went to view the scene again. Crazy you may say, but we did go and before we got to Peldon drizzling rain came on, so we sheltered for a time in the travers of the blacksmiths at the bottom of the hill, not far from Peldon Church. After a little wait we decided to go on just that little bit further to Little Wigborough. The Zeppelin was still guarded as on the previous day, with not quite so many people about but many more I'm sure than Little Wigborough had ever seen before or has since. When my sister and her friend and I decided we had seen enough, we made for the long walk home. We all walked long distances in those days arriving home most likely very tired and footsore, but such was life then.

The War disrupted the fisheries and each smack had to have an official permit which allowed her to fish only in certain areas off the coast. Most were manned by older men and boys and they were often stopped by patrol boats and naval craft. The channel along the Essex coast known as The Swin was sealed off with big steel nets which gave much trouble to the smacks which continued to fish there, sailing about amongst them and often inside them. I remember hearing that the *Elise* and another Wivenhoe smack were once at anchor at night in that part when suddenly they found themselves being dragged along through the water. They had been caught in the wires of two minesweeping trawlers!

Many large warships evidently laid in The Swin and the huge battleship *Dreadnought*, once the pride of our Navy, was flagship there. I believe the famous cruiser *Vindictive* was made ready there for her heroic attack on the Germans at Zeebrugge in 1918.

The *Beatrice* carried on during the War but soon after it, due to my father's illness, she was offered for sale, as were many other smacks at Rowhedge. The *Beatrice* was bought by a young fisherman from Faversham, Kent, who had just been demobilised from the Army and partly paid for her with his gratuity money. He took her away to fish from the Kentish port of Whitstable, where the smacks moored on the hard foreshore, for which I believe they should be specially built. About twenty years ago my son John was sailing on the Kentish coast and called at Whitstable to trace the fisherman, finding him an elderly man who by then owned a fish shop. He said that the poor old *Beatrice* had worked for him for several years but finally broke up on that hard shore.

My father felt lost without a craft of some sort to sail and Mr Leach, who owned the *Reseda* of which he had been captain before the War, let him have a discarded lifeboat from one of this ships. My father and brother brought this boat round from London to Rowhedge and she was converted into a little cruising craft, with a small cabin, and a store and foc'sle. Rigged like a small smack, she sailed fairly well and in the fashion of the smacks, he named her *Reseda* after the yacht he had skippered. My father enjoyed sailing the *Reseda* and often went away in her for a few days "down the river", sailing about amongst his contemporaries in the smacks and yachts, visiting his old haunts and anchorages. When he died, she too was sold and another chapter was sadly ended.

My father at the helm of his cutter rigged, converted ship's boat *Reseda*; the last boat he owned and sailed after selling our smack *Beatrice*. His friend Mr Everitt is near the mast.

Epilogue

THIS book ends in about 1920 but those who have read so far will wish to know the subsequent life of Margaret Barnard.

On leaving school she worked at the clothing factory which was established at Rowhedge, becoming an excellent tailoress and eventually a forewoman in charge of other workers, until her marriage. Needlework skill and pride in her ability to cut well-made garments remained into her late years and she continued to make well-styled and well-fitting clothes for herself throughout her life.

Amongst the many naval vessels which came to the shipyards of Rowhedge, Wivenhoe and Brightlingsea during and immediately after the First World War were numbers of minesweeping and patrol trawlers and drifters; little ships which did so much of the dangerous work of sea warfare. One of these was the drifter H.M.S. *Peterel*, originally fishing from Findochty, Banffshire. Her crew were Royal Naval Reserve men and amongst them was a young sailor, Jack (John) Leather, of a Liverpool family of shipbuilders and marine engineers.

The *Peterel* spent some time repairing damages at the Colne yards and Margaret Barnard and Jack Leather became acquainted, commencing a courtship which ended in their marriage during 1923.

When peace came, the predominantly Scottish crew of the *Peterel* (which included her skipper-owner) invited Jack to return to Scotland with her and fish with them, but he declined and returned to the deep sea ships which had lured him from his school-leaver job as a trainee clerk in a Liverpool shipping office, which he had left early in 1914 to sail in the Allan Line as a seaman in the Atlantic liner *Alsatian*. His father, James Leather, was a marine engineer and his grandfather had been a foreman shipwright of the Mersey Docks and Harbour Board.

At the outbreak of war in 1914, the *Alsatian* became an armed merchant cruiser and those of her crew who were not Royal Naval Reserve men transferred to other ships. Jack joined the liner *Cedric*, on the Liverpool to New York run. In 1915 he enlisted in the Royal Naval Reserve and volunteered for the Dover Patrol; a force which saw considerable action throughout the war.

Jack experienced actions with German submarines and destroyers and witnessed the explosion of a monitor in Dover harbour, all set against the continuous minesweeping, convoys and bombardments of the continental coast. Service in the *Peterel* continued after hostilities ceased, as the mine strewn Channel had to be cleared by hundreds of minesweepers.

On leaving the Navy in September 1919, Jack Leather returned to deep sea ships. For six years he served in the crews of the large cargo steamships *Harmodius, Haliartus, Sea Serpent, Benefactor, Patrician* and *Sea Victory*, voyaging to north and south America, the Baltic, Mediterranean, Cuba and the north Pacific. As the economic slump deepened, more and more merchant ships were laid up and in July 1925 like many contemporaries, he gave up the sea to find work ashore, but always retained a sailor's instincts and outlook.

For some years Jack and Margaret Leather lived in Liverpool, which they both grew to dislike. I was born there on 24th December, 1928, their only child. Liverpool was fascinating to me as a small boy. The liners and other shipping constantly moving on the sullen grey tideway, the excitement of a trip on the ferry steamers to Birkenhead or Wallasey and relative who talked ships as part of everyday life probably set me also on the seemingly inevitable path towards ships and the sea.

The widespread effects of the slump were severe at Liverpool and during 1935 my parents decided to return to north-east Essex. Our household was removed to Rowhedge where we lived in rented accommodation for several months while a new bungalow was built on land my father bought at the nearby, attractively rural village of Fingringhoe.

From 1936 to 1952 we lived there at Fulwood, but as I at first attended school at Rowhedge and had many relatives there, it became my second home and its traditions became mine; a feeling strengthened when I commenced an apprenticeship as a shipbuilding draughtsman at the Rowhedge Ironworks Company shipyard, and worked there for ten years.

My father died during 1952 after a serious illness and as there was little prospect that the very large garden of Fulwood could be kept in good order, the property was sold. My mother wished to return to Rowhedge and purchased a bungalow there, "up the Town Fields", now Rowhedge Road, a short distance out of the village. It was renamed The Knoll after the buoy at the mouth of the entrance to the river Colne and she lived there until 1960, alone after my marriage in 1955. After living at Lowestoft for five years while working at a new shipyard there, I returned to Wivenhoe with my family, convenient for travel to London in connection with my profession of Ship Surveyor.

The sizeable garden of The Knoll also became a burden to my mother and she sold the property during 1960 and bought one of Valkyrie Cottages, number 58, Regent Street, Rowhedge; a small house with a small garden. She lived there for the remainder of her life, surrounded by relations and old friends and especially enjoying frequent visits from her grandchildren, David and Susan Leather.

My mother was always a shrewd observer and found an interest in many things during her long and active life, which included many joys and some reverses which were faced determinedly. Antiques, fine art, history, local and international affairs appealed to her immensely. Seeing a large ship under way, a yacht under sail in a breeze, or a regatta, stirred her enthusiasm for maritime things and although she rarely went afloat, like most with her background, she inherited sea sense from generations of seafaring ancestors. Again, typically, she had great respect for the power of wind and wave; the pleasures and trouble they can bring. She was proud to see her grandchildren, David and Susan, afloat in their sailing dinghies, sailing with my wife and myself in our cruising boats or racing in the regattas. Our removal to Cowes, Isle of Wight, for professional reasons, left her depressed and although rallying bravely, she was in failing health for some time. Preparing for her Christmas visit to Cowes in December 1973, she suffered a severe stroke and died in hospital in Colchester on 21st December 1973.

During 1969 she commenced writing her childhood impressions of life in Rowhedge, encouraged by relatives and friends. She had not previously written for publication but enjoyed this new venture and was delighted at this book's acceptance by the publishers. Unfortunately, she died before its publication.

As she would have wished her book to end typically and cheerfully, here are her descriptions of two of her last expeditions to the Donyland Woods and Heath, where she enjoyed walking throughout her life.

"During late autumn of 1970 we enjoyed almost perfect weather. A friend and I decided to take a walk through the heath to admire the lovely shades of trees and bracken. Never had I seen a time when the bracken had grown to such heights nor shades so beautiful, from yellow to fiery copper. The variations of shading were amazing, and many trees had shed their leaves, enabling us to walk on a carpet of them. What beauty to behold. We thought it all so wonderful and arranged to see it all again the following Sunday, but oh dear, what a change came about during that week. The Indian Summer changed into winter and for a day or so we had hard frosts and heavy snow falls. However, it didn't daunt us and putting on our boots, up to the heath we went as planned, but this time it was "snowland", but still beautiful; snow everywhere. The hard frosts together with snow had caused the holly and oak leaves on the trees to appear like large blobs of snow. We stood and gazed on the scene in admiration, then continued along other paths, and as we walked and looked around us, I walked down a slight unknown incline, and down on the ground I went, myself in one direction and my hat in another! I soon got up off the ground, brushed myself down, none the worse for the skidding. After walking as far as the wood gate we made our way home, leaving the winter wonderland of the heath behind us to enjoy a comfortable fireside and soon the kettle was on and tea made; most enjoyable."

And her last writing for this book:

"Now we will leave the past and take a walk in the present, to brighten the scene with thoughts of spring, and three weeks ago I did just that. On this particular day the sky was so blue and the sun shining so brightly, that I put on my hat and coat and walked up to the heath. Something compelled me to go to see the wonders of springtime. I didn't go into the heath itself, as I had no friends with me, but skirted it and walked up the road that eventually leads to Fingringhoe. I did stray from the road a few times and admired the cherry blossom; a few "cuckoos" were still to be seen, their delicate foliage and tiny white flower sheltering in the undergrowth. With the bluebells in bud and the trees so proud to be bursting out into new leaf, only the oaks were left to come into their glory for the scene to be complete. I stood and gazed, and admired; and in admiration, I found myself saying aloud the first line of a hymn 'My God how wonderful thou art'.

I wended my way home along the nursery path, content in my thoughts and in the beauty I had seen—the beauty of Eternal Spring".

Margaret Barnard, aged twenty-three in 1919.

APPENDIX I

Surnames of Rowhedge families during the period covered by this book.

Adam	Gentry	Robinson
Aldridge	Goodrum	Rose
Allen	Goodwin	Rowe
Bareham	Green	Sargeant
Barnard	Greenleaf	Sargent
Bartholomew	Greenwood	Scarf
Barrel	Harris	Scrutton
Benson	Hillyard	Sebborn
Betts	Holmes	Shaw
Boyston	Houston	Shave
Brown	Howe	Shead
Bugg	Howling	Simons
Burch	Hurst	Smith
Carder	Isom	Southgate
Carter	James	Sparkes
Cheek	Jay	Spinks
Cheshire	Jones	Spitty
Chisnell	King	Spooner
Clarke	Knights	Springett
Cole	Lay	Stiff
Cook	Levett	Taylor
Cooper	Littlebury	Theobald
Cranfield	Marshall	Turff
Cranmer	Martin	Tye
Crosby	Mills	Wade
Cudmore	More	Wainscott
Curle	Moss	Wakeling
Cutts	Motts	Walford
Day	Moulton	Wall
Dove	Owers	Ward
Dyer	Page	Warren
Easter	Parker	Watson
Ennew	Pearman	Webb
Evedley	Pearson	Welham
Everitt	Pepper	White
Fairweather	Pitt	Wilkin
Fale	Porter	Willsmore
Fayer	Potter	Wisbey
Fisher	Powell	Woods
Fisk	Purle	Worsp
Fookes	Richer	

This list may not be complete.

Villagers in the surrounding area also had collective nicknames; Wivenhoe people were referred to as the "Wivenhoe owls", West Mersea inhabitants as "Mersea pirates" while, I suppose because of its situation in the parish of East Donyland, Rowhedgers received the dubious nickname of "Rowhedge Donkeys"! However, they took comfort from the old village saying "Rowhedge shall revive".

The fast yawl *Saionara* heels to a breeze in 1906. She was the first yacht of which my brother, James Barnard, was skipper. She was built to race in the 5 Rating class.

APPENDIX II

Rowhedge smacks and their owners during the period covered by this book.

Name	Port of Registry	Rig	Where Built	Date	Tons	Owner(s)
Adam	Colchester	Cutter	—	—	—	George Cranfield
Alexandra	,,	,,	Rowhedge	1865	22	William Bartholomew
All Serene	—	,,	—	—	—	John Smith
Amelia	—	,,	—	—	—	Ephram Fisher
Aquiline	Colchester	,,	Rowhedge	1867	21	Harry Mills Cook
Beatrice	,,	,,	Wivenhoe	1848	12	James Barnard
Beulah	,,	,,	,,	1821	21	Daniel James
Blanche	,,	,,	—	—	—	Arthur Cranfield
Clara	,,	,,	Rowhedge	—	—	William W. Cranfield
Concord	,,	,,	Colchester	1838	21	David W. P. Martin – Later Ambrose Walford
Dewdrop (Later *Albion*)	,,	,,	,,	—	—	Zac Walford – Later John O. Barnard – C. Brasted
David and Eliza	,,	,,	Jersey	1844	9	Mrs Eliza Page
Deerhound	—	,,	—	—	—	Benjamin Dyer
Druid	Colchester	,,	—	—	—	– Glozier
Elizabeth Ann	,,	,,	—	—	12	Stephen Cranfield
Ellen (Small)	,,	,,	Rowhedge	—	—	Henry Martin
Ellen	,,	,,	Wivenhoe	1886	12	Richard Cranfield
Faith	,,	,,	Rowhedge	1851	22	William Pike Cheek
First Fruits	—	,,	—	—	—	S. Springett
Four Sisters	Colchester	,,	—	—	—	David Martin
Foxhound	,,	,,	—	—	—	– Goodwin
Frolic	—	—	—	—	—	– Brown – Later Henry Martin
Hildegarde	Colchester	Cutter	—	—	—	James Simons
Industry	,,	,,	Burnham	1874	21	Ambrose Walford
Jemima	—	,,	—	—	—	Thomas Allen
Kate and Ann	Colchester	,,	Brightlingsea	1858	11	Isiah Powell
Lily	,,	,,	Rowhedge	—	12	Jonathan Cranfield
Lizzie Maud	—	,,	—	—	—	– Parker
Margaret Ann	—	,,	—	—	—	W. Clarke
Mary	—	,,	—	—	—	David Welham
Neva	Colchester	,,	Rowhedge	—	12	Lemon Cranfield
New Blossom	,,	Ketch	Ipswich	1833	38	Charles Crosby
Paul	,,	Cutter	France	1853	17	Samuel Springett
Qui Vive	,,	,,	Ipswich	1858	18	Benjamin R. Dyer
Rival	—	,,	—	—	—	Thomas Knights
Robert and Ann	Colchester	,,	—	—	—	Henry Sebborn
Running Rein	,,	,,	Wivenhoe	1844	13	John Brown
Snowdrop	,,	,,	Rowhedge	1815	19	William T. Barnard
Sunbeam	,,	,,	—	—	12	William W. Cranfield
Swedenborg	Colchester	,,	Wivenhoe	1855	11	Tabor Cheek – Later H. Martin
Telegraph	,,	,,	Brightlingsea	1866	11	John Cranfield
Thorn	,,	,,	—	—	19	John Spitty
Three Brothers	,,	,,	Brightlingsea	1867	9	Robert Wilkin
Three Sisters	,,	,,	Rowhedge	1789	10	Mrs Jane Taylor
Unity	—	,,	—	—	—	W. James
Varna	Colchester	,,	—	—	—	– Simons
Violet	—	,,	—	—	—	J. Cranfield
William Henry	Colchester	,,	Rowhedge	—	—	Elisha Wade
Wonder	,,	,,	Wivenhoe	1876	12	James Carter
Young Pheasant	,,	,,	Rowhedge	1865	21	Samuel J. Mills
Xanthe	,,	,,	,,	—	—	William Cranfield
(Name Unknown)	—	,,	—	—	—	Abiatha Wilkin

Smacks fitting out in autumn for the winter fisheries. Mr Martin's *Ellen*, C.K.222, with man up mast. Uncle William Cranfield's *Sunbeam* at extreme right.

APPENDIX III

To illustrate the considerable numbers of yachts skippered and manned by men from Rowhedge in the period covered by this book here is a list of those laid up there during the winter of 1896-1897, with the names of their captains, all Rowhedge men. As each carried an average crew of four and often many more, it emphasises the benefits in employment and opportunity yachts offered to the village's seafarers, besides the value of repair and refitting work it brought to the village's yards and their workmen.

This list of forty does not include the many large racing and cruising yachts, also having Rowhedge captains and often complete or partial crews from the village, which were laid up elsewhere, usually because they were too large to be satisfactorily hauled out at the Rowhedge yards.

Antelope. Cutter, Captain Theobald.
Bakaloum. Yawl. Captain Dyer.
Brenda. Cutter, Captain Brown.
Cheetah. Cutter. Captain J. Springett.
Coquette. Schooner. Captain James.
Dawn. Yawl. Captain Blackwell.
Day Dawn. Cutter. Captain Martin.
Deirdre. Cutter. Captain R. Cranfield.
Dove. Yawl. Captain J. Cranfield.
Edwina. Yawl. Captain Hillyard.
Elspeth. Cutter. Captain T. Springett.
Fairlie. Cutter. Captain T. Springett.
Fiona. Cutter. Captain Pearman.
Firecrest. Cutter. Captain P. James.
Glendover. Captain James Barnard.
Glimpse. Cutter. Captain Mark Cutts.
Gudrun. Yawl. Captain Ennew.
Gwendoline. Steam yacht. Captain Sebborn.
Hermia. Yawl. Captain Knights.
Ildegonda. Cutter. Captain J. Springett.

Ilona. Yawl. Captain S. Springett.
Kempion. Steam yacht. Captain Jay.
Lacerta. Schooner. Captain R. Cranfield.
Lady Blanche. Yawl. Captain Watson.
Lassie. Cutter. Captain Wilkin.
Lucina. Cutter. Captain Allen.
Merrythought. Yawl. Captain Simons.
Moina. Captain Carter.
Pathfinder. Steam yacht. Captain Scarfe.
Peregrine. Yawl. Captain Cranmer.
Reindeer. Schooner. Captain Cheek.
Sea Drift. Cutter. Captain Clark.
Spindrift. Cutter. Captain Tye.
Sunset. Schooner. Captain Owers.
Thea. Cutter. Captain Taylor.
Vanadis. Steam yacht. Captain Lay.
Walrus. Steam yacht. Captain Walford.
Wild Wave. Steam yacht. Captain Powell.
Xanthe. Cutter. Captain W. Cranfield.
Zephyr. Cutter. Captain T. Springett.

The *Merrythought* is punching to windward under reefed foresail and trysail, with her bowsprit run in and weathercloths rigged near the helmsman.